STREET CORNER SYMPHONY

STREET CORNER SYMPHONY

Robert L. Glover Jr.

iUniverse, Inc.
New York   Bloomington

STREET CORNER SYMPHONY

iUniverse books may be ordered through booksellers or by contacting:

iUniverse
1663 Liberty Drive
Bloomington, IN 47403
www.iuniverse.com
1-800-Authors (1-800-288-4677)

ISBN: 978-0-595-36701-6 (pbk)
ISBN: 978-0-595-81124-3 (ebk)

Printed in the United States of America

Contents

It is December 31ˢᵗ, it is 11:30 p.m., it is also New Years Eve, and the year is 1993. I am 38 years old, and I do not expect to live to see the New Year of 1994, and I am okay with that. You see, I am sitting in a crack house, and I am waiting for someone to come in and kill me, or I kill them. I have a gun, and some people for company. Also sitting here is my nephew Omar and my girlfriend Sandi. You see, we have been making too much money for the people we deal for, Lamont and Top-cat, so these young boys from across Girard Avenue from 15ᵗʰ and Stiles Streets are going to take over our drug house, or kill us in the process. The people we work for have given us these guns to protect ourselves and their crack with. Nevertheless I suspect that they are out partying and enjoying the New Years Eve festivities somewhere while we are left here on our own. If there is any dying to be done tonight, let us be the ones to die, because to the drug dealers that we work for we are expend-able. Nevertheless, we are somewhat prepared for the thugs who are coming to kill us, for we were warned by Worm, the local loan shark, that these nameless thugs were planning a New Years eve attack. I owed Worm $300.00, so his motive may have been to protect me until I got my welfare check so that I could pay him off, or maybe he was genuinely concerned, I tend to believe it was the former. Worm was really scared himself; he told me that by just warning me was risking his own life. So when a man like Worm with that much power in the neighborhood is scared, we should be scared too. He told me I could expect them to be wearing black hoods, and they were going break into the house and going to kill everything in the house, so I sent my young nephew Jay to his grandmother's house, there was no need for him to also get killed also. The drug dealers from Stiles Street came to the house the week before, and asked to speak to me, we were making a million dollars a year for the drug dealers that we worked for. So the drug dealers from Stiles Street wanted a piece of the action, everybody wanted a piece of the action, I told them no, and they said that they would be back. So I forgot about it until Worm warned us, I knew this was some serious shit we were involved in. So for warned, here we sit, huddled in the front room, underneath the big picture window with our backs to the wall, we are even more prepared for this ambush than you might think.

We have been given plywood to board the windows up, courtesy of the drug dealers. So we boarded up every window in the house, all ten of them, I know because I counted them, and we wait, with a pack of drugs to sell, and fear gripping us all. Me, I have to wonder if I will have the nerve to shoot someone if they come into the house tonight. I had never up to that point in my life shot at anyone before, I wondered about everyone else in the room, would they pull the trigger if those guys came busting in because the lock on the door was flimsy and would not stop them from getting in. This 357 magnum handgun was as big as shit, Omar had a 350 handgun, and we had a 22 caliber automatic handgun, so we were prepared. I do not think the lock could have stopped them anyway no matter how strong it was if they really wanted to get in. With each hit of the crack all of us except Omar, he only drank beer, which he had, grew more paranoid; will I shoot myself by mistake? So we wait, no words are spoken, each of us dealing with our fate in their own way, with their own thoughts.

For me it is a time to reflect on how I got into this shit in the first place. I remember, as a young man of 21 years old, leaving Lincoln University with such promise, to work at The Institute for Behavioral Research, in Silver Spring Maryland and I remember how proud my parents were, I was the chosen one, the one who would take their dreams and my family's dreams out into the world, groomed to succeed, for their sake. Out of the 10 children they had, I was expected to do well, a hell of a load to carry, a load I did not want to bear, so here I am, living a life gone bad. It is getting closer to 12:00 p.m., the New Year of 1994, and I believe my life will soon be over, and that it will end tonight. And I am okay with that as long as I can get high. So we load up our crack pipes, Sandi and me, and my nephew Omar drinks his beer, and we salute the New Year, I geuss it was some where around midnight, but I could not be sure. There was no Dick Clark here, no Times Square and no countdown for the ball to drop. Oh there used to be, when I was a normal person before drugs, but not anymore. This is my life now, this is my destiny now, or so I think. As the smoke from the pipe envelops the room, in the darkness, your mind plays tricks on you. You see your whole life, spread out in that cloud of drugs, you see family members, you see friends, you see memories of high school, college, and just growing up in pain. But how did I get here? I try to reflect on that, but my drug clouded mind does not want to deal with the past, with the reality of my situation or were my choices have lead me, so I take another hit of crack, and continue to wait to die, like the Notorious B.I.G. says, I'm Ready To Die. So I think for a minute, how did this shit happen, I geuss I have to go back to the beginning of my story. And that is where I have to start.

ACT ONE:
IN THE BEGINNING …

1

A Difficult Childhood, Growing Up In The Sixties.

Where does a person start when they are attempting to reflect on their life, and attempting to put their life down on paper? Would a person start at the beginning of their life, would they start at the middle of their life, or would they start at the end of their life? And where would you start if it were you writing your life story? I guess that this is a question we all must ask ourselves, and hope that this question is addressed before we pass from this sphere of existence to the next sphere of existence. Nevertheless, how does a person begin to deal with all of the anger, all of the ugliness of who they are? How does a person deal with the self hatred and doubt that drives them, the kind of doubt that rides them like a monkey on their backs each and every day of their lives? How does that person as well deal with the beauty that each of us is given in our lives? Also how does each of us deal with the wonder of our existence? How do we deal with an existence that seeks to balance itself everyday of our lives? That is more than most of us wish to do; in fact we actively seek to avoid these questions as much as possible. Is this fair? Hell no, but it's what we have to work with, and work with it we must. You see, we have no choice, or say so in the matter. Life is the greatest choice that we are given that is not ours to make. No one came here on his or hers own accord, no one said I think this thing down here on this planet is cool; I want to be a part of that, no that's not the way it happened. That choice was made for us by our God and our parents, and other factors beyond our control, so here we are, now what? That is the cruel paradox upon which all of our existence is

3

based; a life of choices began without choice. So this is the analysis of a life with choice that began without choice. I often ask myself, would anyone if given the choice choose to be born, but is that a fair question to ask someone? We must all look at our lives with our own sense of understanding, which is all that we can do, so I look at my life within the realm of my understanding.

My Family:

I was born in the 1950's, the era of the baby boomers, 1954 to be exact. Nevertheless did I realize that from these humble beginning would emerge so much self doubt? That from these humble beginnings I would never have imagined that I would develop so much self persecution and raw self hatred, and that it would lead me to the path that my life has taken to this point in time. I don't remember much about my early childhood, I don't know if that is good or bad, but my first memories of my life where memories of unhappiness. Not the kind of unhappiness that comes from not being loved let me make that perfectly clear, my mother loved me with all of her heart, as well as my father in his own way, and that is something I did not realize until I had grown up is that we don't all love the same way. Each of us has a unique capacity for love that is different from each other. My grandmothers loved me on both sides, I was fortunate to know my great grandmother, Willie Johnson. I was lucky to know my grandfathers on both sides of the family, Lonnie Ballard and John Palmer. I was very lucky to grow up in my Nana's house that was the first house I knew growing up as a child; you see times were a little bit easier at her house in terms of food availability, a little more money to spend. My Nana and my great grandmother would always give me money, I would go up on Ridge Avenue to Perry's five and ten cent store and buy all sort of wonderful things. Perry's was like a Woolworth five and ten cent store, back then Ridge Avenue was alive and bustling with businesses and shops, you could get almost anything there. They had Jewish run shoe stores, the food market, the fish stores and Perry's 5&10 cent store anchoring it all along with the Big Store. Back then there was back then no need to go downtown, you could get all that you needed on Ridge Avenue. I used to love the Big Store it was where you could purchase Chuck Taylor's sneakers for twelve dollars and John Smith sneakers for eight dollars and fifty cents. John Smiths were the poor mans Chuck Taylor, you wore them if you could not afford Chuck Taylor's. Chuck Taylor's were the sneaker of my generation, just as Nikes are the sneaker of the present generation. All of the National Basketball Association players wore Chuck Taylor canvas sneakers and so did we. Man, it was an amazing thing to see with all of the Jewish merchants that were on Ridge Avenue, now it is just a desolate stretch of avenue, how time changes things for the worst sometimes. I remember that I would buy gold fish from Perry's they never lived long, but they were mines, bought with my money. Bringing them home in that plastic bag and putting them oh so carefully into the little glass bowl that came with them, they were my first pets.

Nevertheless my in-laws were very dysfunctional, they loved each other in a strange way, and taught us this strange way to love, were you love a family member one minute and hate them the next. The constant arguing between my great grandmother and her daughters was very strange, but I knew it wrong. My great grandmother and my grandfather were two characters, they love to play like they were arguing with each other, and they would fight about almost anything. I remember when Ronald Reagan was running for president the first time, my great grandmother asked if my grandfather was going to vote republican this year. He responded that he was a democrat, and being a democrat why would he vote for Ronald Reagan; she said to him in jest, "You must be an Alabama Reagan nigger". My great grandmother Willie Johnson would lie up in her bedroom on the second floor of that house and it was as if she was a queen holding court, she would dispense money from her trusty change purse, a dime at a time. I would sneak downstairs and drink her citrate of magnesia from out of the refrigerator, it tasted like seven up soda, but it moved your bowels unlike anything else. My Aunt Marion was quite a character too, she would smoke her cigarettes and she had the back second floor bedroom. Once she caught me sneaking and smoking her cigarettes, so she punished me by making me smoke a whole package of cigarettes, twenty in all. I got so sick, and then they took it a step further as my grandmother Nana had arrived by that time. They told me to eat this chicken, and told me it was roasted rat meat, I got so sick from the cigarettes and the fake rat meat that I never wanted to smoke again, it was very effective to say the least.

My Aunt Marion had a daughter, Ruth and she had her family, they were my first cousins, Chucky, Kim and Robin Denise, we called her Robin Denise as not to confuse her with my sister Robin. Once Ruthie as we called her took her children and me to a baseball game at the old Connie Mack stadium to see the Philadelphia Phillies play a doubleheader, we had to walk back to Broad Street from 22nd and Lehigh Avenue after the ball game to catch the subway train home, there were all of these people, walking up Lehigh Avenue to the Broad Street subway. There were white people and black people in the crowd, and everyone felt safe walking together, it was what people did in those days when the ballgame let out, it is certainly different now. With all the crime, death and destruction, you take your life into your hands if you walk down Lehigh Avenue now. There is a church on Lehigh Avenue where Connie Mack stadium once stood, a reminder of how things change.

I got to spend time with my cousins on my father's side; there was James Cooper, Chalmers Williams, and Jimbo. We called Chalmers Moot. Moot would drink a lot of wine, I guess that you could say that he was an alcoholic; it was my first encounter with someone who had a substance abuse problem. Except back then, it wasn't called a substance abuse problem; he was just called a drunk. And it was not yet politically correct for society to deal with the issue of alcoholism in any way except the way that they dealt with it I suppose. Nevertheless I learned to love Moot and we all learned to forgive him for his shortcomings, you see it wasn't really his fault; he was a relic of the fifties, that time when black men would turn to alcohol to ease their pains, to deal with a society that shunned them. The realization that you are less than a man, the realization that you don't measure up to the society that you live in, the realization that you cannot amount to anything, or ever be given the chance to do so must have been devastating for our black race and especially the black men. It was only natural that they turned to drugs and alcohol to drown their sorrows. I am in no way making excuses for the behavior of my cousin Moot, but I am simply trying to understand the demons that he wrestled with that led him to make the choices that he made in his life. I am trying to relate to you how these demons can be passed from one generation to another, the demons of self doubt, the demons of self hatred and the demons of racism can be crippling to say the least. I now understand how the story of Moot relates to me and to all people who learn to doubt themselves as human beings. It is a personal capacity that separates us not only from each other but from every other form of life on this sphere we call our own. No, my unhappiness came from an early realization that something was wrong, I could not put my finger on it but I knew it was there. Always there, lurking in my life my, my self doubt feeds off it, my self image damaged by it, and shaped by it. They say there is a destiny for all of us, predetermined by fate, hard wired by God. A path that each of us must follow whether we want to or not. They also say that life is either a journey to a destination, or a destination that is defined by the journey we take, each of these are up to the individual to determine. And I don't really know which one mines was or is, except to say I am here, and this is what I must deal with. I was groomed to be a leader, but I did not want the responsibility that comes with leadership. I could speak the words but the commitment was not there, I could speak the words rhetorically to inflame the masses to positive ends, but I did not want the responsibility that came with being a leader, so I ran and hid in drugs and found refuge in them, it proved to my undoing.

So like I said it all started very sweet, but went sour very fast. Good memories where matched by bad memories as life became a game of cat and mouse, the good trying to outdo the bad, no I guess you could say trying to equalize each other, and I guess that's all fate or life or whatever you want to call it ever promised us, it's just that some have more of either and maybe that's what determines what we are and who we are. They say that I ran away from home at age four, in 1958, my grandmother and mother told me I put my hat and coat on and rolled,

I was mad about something and being only four years old, I ran away. They also told me that a Philadelphia police officer bought me back home. I had made it to the corner of my block, which was at 15th and Ogden streets, almost to Girard Avenue before I was spotted; my parents never knew that I left. That I made it that far, without being hit by a car was divine intervention. I really don't remember any of this but it was my first rebellious move, and certainly not my last. Much of my early life is hazy, I see pictures of me in first grade, and I went to a Catholic school.

All I can remember from Catholic school was that the nuns would crack your knuckles with a ruler when you misbehaved. I do not remember if it was done with malice, but the nuns were sure to go to that ruler when they thought that you acted up. Nevertheless, that was also my first introduction to religion, through those nuns. We were required to attend Catholic services on Sunday and if you missed service on Sunday the nuns would crack your knuckles with that ruler. But the next thing I remember is moving from my grandmother's house and getting a house of our own, you see we lived with our grandmother Nana from the time I can remember, until we moved to Toronto Street in 1961, Nana had helped my dad buy that house for us. It was in the winter time during a blizzard, by that time our family had grown to seven, the twins and my baby sister would come after we moved. We were one of the first black families in the neighborhood. I remember that our house was owned by an elderly white couple that had passed away. There were these beautiful drawings on the wall throughout the house when we took down the wallpaper, drawings from the 19th century. The drawings depicted scenes of boxers, of life situations and of everyday living from that era. People working, delivering milk, and doing other jobs related to the early 19th century, like an immigrant tapestry, the story of the Irish people, which is when I became interested in art, I wanted to be an artist after I saw those pictures, and they really inspired me. I wondered who those people was who were portrayed in the artwork, what were they like, where did they come from, and most importantly, how did they get there? I never got the answer to those questions because we removed those pictures from the wall, we washed them off, and they were to be lost forever. Now I know how my ancestors must have felt, to be a culture wiped from a wall, no longer to exisit, gone forever.

I can also remember spending our first holiday on Toronto Street, the Christmas tree, a live green Christmas tree, not that fake crap that they have today. The trips downtown to see the enchanted Christmas Village at Gimbels Brothers department store, to sit on Santa Claus's knee, he was very real to us back then and tell him what you wanted for Christmas, then he would reach into that sack and give you a gift, it was like an early Christmas, one year I got a Zorro cape and sword, and another year I got a James Bond briefcase. Of course the highlight of the trip was going to see the Enchanted Christmas village, it was well enchanting, all of the shops and the holiday scenes everything was automated. The magic that it invoked, of seeing those figures move around by themselves was so delightful to a small child like myself, the light shops, the whole thing was like nothing I had ever seen before, it was truly magic.

Then I remember the racism that came with the move. We went swimming at the Huntington Park swimming pool which was at Old York Road and Huntington Park avenues. The young white children my age saying when they saw us "Run, here comes the Hershey Kids ", I never knew until years later that was a racial slur, they were talking about the color of our skin, because to them we looked like the color a Hershey bar. I was even at that early age a little offended by being called a candy bar, and by other children not wanting to play with me. I wondered why we could not just play together, they were children, we were children, and I had no idea that the color of my skin was so important to some people. I guess that children learn from their parents and that shapes who they are and what they think. Nevertheless I remember as a child going to the doctor and having to wait in a separate waiting room, having to deal with race related issues as a child but not really understanding what was going on. That this kind of racism was happening here in the enlightened north still blows my mind even today. These things were happening in the year 1962, but they were and they shaped me and forged the self doubt that I still struggle with. I never felt comfortable with myself, with who I was, I was definitely suffering from an identity crisis, I was very quiet and withdrawn, I always felt that other people were better than me. We had to wear brogans, these were boots that only poor boys wore, they lasted forever and my father would make them last even longer by getting taps put on the soles of the boots. You could not get rid of those boots, they lasted about a year of hard wear, we used to make that trip down to the Old Shoe City store that was located on Arch Street to get those brogans, and I hated those shoes. I always felt that I was not dressed as good as everybody else was, so I felt inadequate, but I kept these feelings of inadequacy to myself. As a black person growing up in the sixties I was made to fell inadequate by the society at large.

I remember Little Stevie Wonder made his debut on American Bandstand, he played "Fingertips", there was some music going on then, the year was 1962 and the sound of soul was everywhere, to see that little blind boy who looked like me playing music was very uplifting. There were the Five Stair Steps and other groups that made hit after hit. I remember that I once wanted to be in the talent show at Gillespie Jr. High School, I would sing this song by The Five Stair Steps over and over in the mirror while my brother Douglas watched me, we both knew that I did not have the courage to perform it in front of all my peers but it was great fun. Nevertheless it was not all bad growing up; there were holidays, birthdays, and we were a close knit family that just got bigger and bigger and bigger. We ended up with twelve people living in a three bedroom house. It was very tight, and I shared a room with five brothers, we had three sets of bunk beds, and we had three dressers. My brothers and I lived in a nine by twelve foot room, it was very crowded to say the least, but you get used to it. You got used to never having enough space to breathe it seemed, and when my brothers started to smoke, it was really unbearable. My mom did the best she could as well as my dad in his own way, but my mom always seemed like she was raising us by herself. Nevertheless, no matter how bad things got, my mother always loved us with all of her heart. My dad was sometimes never home, and the food would run out, the coal would run out and the heat would run out, so we learned to burn old furniture, anything that would burn we put in the coal furnace for heat. Then there was the food we would get from welfare, I do not have to remind anyone about the government cheese, the pork and the beef in the can or the powdered milk. And the peanut butter that was so thick when you opened the can and all of the oil was at the top, you had to stir it to be able to make sandwiches, and that is right, back then peanut butter came in a can. These were staples in our house and my mother knew how to hook that canned pork up with some rice and onions.

We used to have just enough money to buy a couple of fifty pound bags of coal to heat the house with when we could not afford a ton of coal. We would purchase the coal from the coal yard right there at Broad and Indiana Avenue. I accepted the responsibility at an early age to tend to that fire, and learned from my dad to keep the house warm when he wasn't there. To bank the fire at night, so that it would not go out, to keep the radiator full of water to humidify the air and to put the ashes out on trash day which was every Monday, I took pride in that task, and did it well. I was the master of the heat in our house. Sometimes there was no coal and nothing to burn, on those occasions we were cold, and I mean it got real cold sometimes, where you could see your breath when you breathed, so we would go outside and gather wood that we found until we could afford a delivery of coal. We had a coal bin and the truck would pull up, we would take out the cellar window and the coal man would tilt the truck and pour in the coal, sometimes it would be a ton, sometimes it would be a half of a ton, sometimes it would be a quarter of a ton. That coal dust would be all over the basement, but at least we had heat, I would play in the coal bin during the summer when we had no use for it, it was weird, but that is the way that it was. I always imagined as a child that there were hidden tunnels under my house; it could be kind of spooky down there, and even so, I loved the musty smell of the cellar. I guess that is weird too, but there must be other people who loved the smell of a musty cellar.

We had this living room furniture that was covered in plastic, I remember when the salesman came out to the house to measure the sofa, loveseat and the chair, it seemed so space age at the time, but there were drawbacks, the plastic would get extremely hot in the summertime, it would stick to your skin if your sat on it. This was the era before air conditioning, we were lucky if we had a fan to keep us cool and the plastic would also get very yellow once it got old, it made the furniture look horrible. Nevertheless, that is what everyone was doing and back then you had to keep up the Jones, or at least give the illusion of keeping up with the Jones. It is amazing to me now how we would do things because everyone else was doing it, we do that as a society today, someone sets the trend and we all follow like lemmings that are jumping off a cliff, no thought of individual thinking!

We also had a family that lived down the street from us on Toronto Street, they had a piano in their living room, we would sit in that living room and the father who was a preacher would play gospel and we would sing along with him and his children. I was the same age as his children and we would all sing, this one song comes to mind, and it went like this "Back to the dust, back to the dust, back to the dust we must go. God made the father, God made the son, back to the dust we must go". We would sing that song all night, and it was something else. We had a close knit block on Toronto Street, we all looked out for each other, the parents for the children and if you did something wrong, they would punish you and tell your parents that they did it. Your parents would not get mad at them for correcting you either, and you might get another whipping from your parents if the offense warranted it. You cannot do that now, it has really changed, if you hit someone's child now, even if he or she is in the wrong, the parents might shoot you, we have forgotten that it takes a village to raise a child, we as parents need all of the help that we can get.

Hershey Park:

There were not all bad times, there were some good times on Toronto Street also, and the family would go to Christmas, Easter, and Thanksgiving at my grandmother Nana's house. We would have these wonderful cookouts in Fairmount Park, my father would be on the grill, and our whole family would show up, in-laws, cousins, aunts and uncles, my mother would make this potato salad that was out of this world.

My great grandmother, Willie Johnson, along with my grandmother Nana, would organize a bus excursion to Hershey Park each summer. We would go up to that park every year on a Saturday and we would ride every ride there was; the roller coaster was my favorite. At that time in the sixties Hershey Park had the highest wooden roller coaster in the world, you would get on this contraption and you could hear the chain as it pulled your car up to the first dip at the top. It seemed as if I was on the top of the world, the people looked so small, so insignificant, almost like ants. Then there was a silence, it could not have been more than a moment, but it seemed to last for an eternity, then there was the creak of the cars, the groan of the chain, and the release and you were off, down that first dip at break neck speeds. The wind would be in your face, your lunch was about to be thrown up as your stomach lurched forward. The screams that came form your lungs, although you could not be sure that it was your screams, hell everyone was screaming in fear and in delight as the coaster dipped and dodged. You almost lost your seat as gravity worked to keep you in your seat and pull you out at the same time, then there was the fear, but you overcame it with youthful exuberance. I do not think that I ever saw my parents and grandparents on the roller coaster and after I got older and became a parent I realized why, it was too damn scary! Memories of my Nana and my parents playing skee ball, back then it only cost a nickel and them winning all of the tickets in the world it seemed like, only to redeem them for these horrible cheap prizes, the same as you do down in Wildwood New Jersey on their boardwalk now. Although the prizes might have been cheap, they were priceless to us then.

They had an arcade where you could watch old kinescope movies that were made in the 1920's for a penny. You could get old movie hero's postcards for a penny, like the Lone Ranger, Roy Rodgers, Hopalong Cassidy, Gene Autry and so many others. The ten dollars that my grandmother gave me would seem to last all day. We would have so much fun as a family, for so little money, my mother and all of the females in my family would cook fried chicken. They would be up all night cooking that chicken, we had such a large family, and the smell of that chicken would waffle through my grandmother's house.

The coolers were filled with the ham and cheese sandwiches, the fried chicken wrapped in aluminum foil along with the fruit and the sodas. We could not sleep anyway, and would be up all night in anticipation of the adventure we would share the next day. At eight in the morning the buses would arrive and we knew that it was on, as the rest of my family had began to arrive before then, by seven that morning, my cousins, my aunts and uncles, and everyone else would arrive. We would load up the bus and then we were off, taking that ride to Hershey Pennsylvania, it seemed like it took forever, but it was not that far away looking back on it. Once we were in Hershey Pa., we had to drive through the town to get to the park, and the streets were lined with street lamps that were shaped like Hershey Kisses, with the aluminum foil and everything. Of course you could take a tour of the Hershey chocolate plant and they would give you a free Hershey Bar once you completed the tour. We would stop at Howard Johnson's Motor Lodge, now how many people even remember Howard Johnson's Motor Lodge? To most people Howard Johnson might be the name of their neighbor and not a motor lodge. Nevertheless we would stop there and it would be ice cream for everyone, ten cones, which was one for each child. Once when we were on our way back, we stopped at Howard Johnson's and my parents bought the ice cream cones, except there was an extra ice cream cone, which meant someone was missing. They took a head count and my younger brother William was missing, we had left him at Hershey Park, and my parents were frantic, along with my grandparents and grandmother and everybody else. They called back to Hershey Park and sure enough my brother was with the park rangers, my mother was relieved. So as soon as we got back to Philadelphia, my father and grandfather rented a car and drove all the way back to Hershey Park to get their child. We waited all night for them to get back with my brother, nobody slept, but when the dawn arose, there he was, our William. We were so relieved, there was so much family love that night, those trips to Hershey Park were golden to us, and they gave us memories that we all share, and will never forget.

So I learned at an early age to be responsible and right from wrong, it was up to me to put these lessons to use and sometimes I did not. I also learned that I was not what you would call street smart; I learned at an early age that your own kind would take advantage of you. There was a time when I would clean the house of my grandmother Mom-mom's sister, my great Aunt Carrie. She would give a nominal fee for a lot of work because that's how it was back then. You see people from that generation were bought up on hard work, and believed that you work for what you get, a lesson that is lost on our young people today. Anyway she gave me the money, three dollars and I was holding on to it for a trip to the carnival that weekend. I carried it with me everywhere I went, so some older guys were riding by on a bike. I was at 17th and Westmoreland streets; they were about three or four years older than me. They asked if they could see my money, sure I said and gave it to them, they rode off with my money, I just stood there for a long time, first knowing they would come back, then hoping they would come back, then wishing they would come back, they never did of course. So I learned to keep my money in my pockets, and that you see with your eyes not with your hands. From this incident a basic distrust of people was born in me, one I would deal with the rest of my life. I also remember how lucky I was to have my grandmother and grand-father on my mother's side live right around the corner from me on Broad Street, their names was Drucilla Williams and John Palmer. I would always venture around to her house to see her and my grandfa-ther, she would always serve me tea with milk, I hated tea with milk, I would have rather had lemon, but I would drink it anyway out of respect for her. She would also make this stewed chicken, she never fired her chicken and she cooked with these wonderful cast iron pots and pans. My Mom-mom as we used to call her was very religious and she attended church every Sunday, but I always felt as if I never really knew her for some reason. I could never put my finger on it but it seemed like we were always strangers although I am sure that she loved me in her own way.

Another lesson I learned at a young age is when myself and my best friend Ernest Lee went to the circus at Lighthouse Field, they would come every summer and stay for a week or two. My best friend's nick-name was Hymn-time, I had no idea what it meant and I still do not, that is just what his family called him. So we were finally old enough to go by ourselves. We got there, and while deciding what we were going to ride, this game barker convinced us to try our luck on one of those rigged games; we quickly fell under his spell, and ended up losing everything we had, including our carfare back home. We went to a policeman, and bought him back to the dishonest game barker, and told us there was nothing he could do. Disillusioned, and dirty, we prepared for the long walk home, we were forced to drink out of a horse trough where they watered the horses, and then we walked back home, and I always held something against game barkers after that. I had no idea that they made money out of taking advantage of people, I had no idea that the way of the world was like that. I learned once again that the world is not a perfect place, and it was also an early lesson that people would do anything for money; even trick a few innocent children. From at this point on in my life I really believed that all people were dishonest, little did I know that this was not the case. It is funny how you can learn things as a child that can determine the way you think and the way you interact with other people for the rest of your life. I guess that is why early childhood and what you learn as child is so important in determining how you grow up and what you think about and how you act as an adult. Children and their impressionable minds are ready to soak up every experience whether good or bad, these experiences go a long way in determining the path that the child will take later on in life. Will the child become a good person or a bad person; we just do not realize the power that we weld over these little people that we encounter.

I also remember the first encounter I had with someone who was mentally ill. As children you learn to make fun of people who are different, people who do not fit the mold of what is perceived as normal, so when we meet someone that does not fit the mold, we make fun of him or her. We were at Teen Haven, it was facility that was located at the top of the block I grew up on, and it was at Broad and Toronto Street. The people at Teen Haven were all white and not much older than we were, but they cared about us. They were passionate about making a difference to us by giving us an alternative to gangs and hanging out in the streets. We would go there after school and make cookies, watch television and play all sorts of games. I remember that I was watching the Mod Squad over there one night when Linc got shot, I almost died, and I really got into television back then. I loved Star Trek, It Takes a Thief, and The Man from Uncle, but besides television they gave us a safe haven when there were not many safe havens for young black children. We would go to their camp in the summer and they never asked for anything from us, just that we respect them and the building by leaving the violence outside.

So anyway, we were at Teen Haven one summer day and this older black guy was walking up Broad Street. He approached us and said that he had a nice shiny bicycle that he wanted to give away, all we had to do was answer this question he would ask us, and the question was "are you Dennis the menace". So there were about eight of us there and we were all trying to win the bike, being poor a new bike was a luxury that most of us could not afford. So he asked us the question, "Are you Dennis the menace", and we all answered yes I am Dennis the menace. Then the game really began, we had to say it like him, repeat the question just like he said it, "Are you Dennis the menace". Nevertheless he kept changing the way he said it, emphasizing different words, repeating it different ways, saying are you Dennis the menace, hunching his shoulders and moving different parts of his body and getting very animated. We tried to duplicate it just as he said it each time and each time it did not meet his approval. This went on for over a half hour, finally he said that no one would win the bike because we could not repeat the phrase good enough for him, and he continued on down Broad street, we were all heartbroken. As I look back on this episode now, we could never have won the bike because there was no bike; he was just a crazy old man having fun with a group of children so poor that we were willing to do or say anything to get a bike.

Nevertheless I did get a bike, it was a tank as old bikes were called back then, a two wheeler with those thick tires, and someone had left it over my grandmother Nana's house. My dad ended up riding it home one night when he was drunk, and I had my bike, I was both ashamed of it and proud that I finally had a bike because all of my friends had new bikes. I also had to peddle it very hard to keep up with my fiends when I rode it, they had ten speed bikes, I had a no speed bike, but I rode it nonetheless, it was all that I had.

We were bused as children to a white school for educational equality in 1964 to schools in the northeastern part of the city. There, we were looked at as being different, and the whites up in the northeast were not used to seeing black people in their neighborhoods at all. So a few of my friends and I stole a small amount of toys not having any money to but them, I wanted to get my sister Robin something for her birthday. The owner of the store and the police were able to come to Clara Barton school and pick us up, we were the only black students there, That was pretty embarrassing to say the least, when my father found out, he made me stay in the house for a month, I would have rather taken the beating than have to be confined to that small bedroom that I shared with my five brothers. I would sit up there everyday after school for hours by myself, it was horrible, but it taught me never to steal from a store again. I guess that it was embarrassing to my parents to have to go up to the school after I was suspended; I guess that I just reinforced the opinion that whites had of us anyway. They treated us like social outcast and we were totally out numbered, recess was a trip, they were just going through the motions mandated by the United States Government. The year was 1964, and to say that we were not treated well at Clara Barton elementary school was an understatement. This world in the northeastern part of the city of Philadelphia was like a new world to us, a world outside our realm of understanding and our ability to comprehend; it was different in sights and sounds. I remember the first time that I missed the bus at fifteenth and Clearfield streets and I walked to school, I did not dare go back home, it seemed like I was walking to another country or something. It seemed like a far away place, or like another planet, after I grew up I learned it was not as far away as I thought, but I will explain that later.

We were tolerated by the adults at Clara Barton School and ridiculed by the children, we just did not fit in, and if anything good did come of it, it was that we were exposed to white people and them to us. Eating lunch was really difficult because the white children had money to eat lunch and we would have to eat the free lunch that they provided for poor children, and of course the white kids looked down on us for that. At recess and after lunch, there was nobody to play with, although I did have a few friends that were white, one was named Neal and his dad drew this picture of Batman and Robin, I will never forget that picture, I wanted to draw too after I saw that picture. Nevertheless it was a better school, better books, better lunch and better teachers, even at an early age I could see that. We were so innocent, I remember when a friend of mine, Cynthia was hit by a car at Fifteenth and Clearfield Streets while we waited for the buses, she ran out from between two parked buses, the driver who hit her never saw her. I remember that that he stroked her hair as she lay in the street waiting for an ambulance to come, thank god she was alright. But what hurt the most was that we were forced to leave our neighborhood school, Kinderton elementary school, to go to another school, it did not make sense to me even at that early age.

I remember that my mother was a school crossing guard at 15th and Allegheny Avenue; I remember how proud I was of her, always standing and manning her post. I can remember my mother looking out for all of the young children in the neighborhood, her ten children and everyone else's. I always felt safe when I was walking to school. Just knowing that she was out there, knowing that my mother would be out there no matter how cold it got, through the summer heat and the rain, she was always there. God how I love my mother, she is the most important woman in the world to me, always will be. I just could never explain it; she was always there for me, no matter what.

1968:

I could never explain to you the year 1968, it was probably, no it was the most difficult year of my life. There was so much going on, I was fourteen years old and this year would change my life and America forever. There were the assignations of Dr. Martin Luther King Jr. and Robert Fitzgerald Kennedy. The Civil Rights Movement was in full swing with daily pictures of black people being abused on television, there were the pictures of the water hoses turned on black people, the police and their dogs attacking black people, which is the memory of the sixties that I have and of course there was the Vietnam War.

There were the riots that followed the death of Dr. King, there was the black power movement and then there were John Carlos and Tommie Smith. After winning the gold and the bronze medals in the 200 meters race, they thrust their black gloved fist to the sky as they received their gold medals at the Mexico City Olympic Games. Being only fourteen at the time, I was still experiencing puberty, but there was so much excitement going on, and so much sorrow. For I lived through the failure of America to make things right for its entire people, I lived through the last chance in my lifetime for the racist dogma that had permeated this country and left it's foul stench on all Americans to end in justice. I saw that the American Dream was still a nightmare for many of its citizens. All this was going on as I struggled to find my place in my world and in their world. I saw George Forman vilified by black America for waving a tiny American Flag after winning the heavyweight gold medal in boxing. I saw so many mixed signals and mixed messages as the confusion of this country clashed with the confusion as to who I was in this country. Was it a racist country, separate yet unequal? Or was it is a just country were the color o f your skin did not matter, where all men were created equal? As I played tag in the summer, I was becoming somewhat aware that the purity of my childhood was coming to an end and the society that I lived in was going to force me to deal with it's iniquities whether I wanted to or not. Things were not as they seemed, or not as they were supposed to be, or not what they were promised to be.

As the sixties drew to an end, it was almost like there was no sense of morals or decency in the country; we were morally bankrupt as a country. It was the beginning of the "me" generation, me first, whoever has the most toys wins. The Vietnam War was on television nightly. The horrors and atrocities were played out right before our eyes, right with our evening dinner. There was also the racial injustice that was festering like a sore that wouldn't heal. Nevertheless it was an exhilarating time to be alive, and also a dangerous time to be alive. The murders of the three civil rights workers in Mississippi, the murder of

Meager Eavers, then the cascade of violence that became the sixties, the burning of Columbia Ave right here in Philadelphia in 1964, that the North part of Philly never recovered from. The burning and looting in Watts, in California, the country was like a keg of racial dynamite, ready to explode, Detroit also burned it was insanity. We used to have a National Guard armory at Broad and Susquehanna Avenue, we would run to the top of Toronto and Broad Street to cheer the tanks as they came down Broad Street and rumbled toward the armory, not knowing that the real reason they were there was as a deterrent to any threat or perceived violence in the black community.

But there were moments of beauty, like the Jewish involvement in the civil rights struggle. The Jewish community more than any other, with the horror of the Holocaust still fresh in their minds, took up the struggle for black to gain equal rights in this country, something that had not happened before or has not happened since. Nevertheless as the decade of the sixties closed, I began to become a man. I went to Gillespie Jr. High School. That was all a blur. With gang violence and all, you took your life in your hands crossing a different gang turf's just to get to school. I then attended Simon Gratz High School, also a forgettable experience. The best thing I got form attending Simon Gratz was that I was able to run track and cross country. Running cross country gave me confidence that I could compete athletically, and challenged me to finish the course every time we had a meet. Running track was a good learning experiences and it provided me a chance to mix with other young men who were not about drugs and violence, just competition. Still the streets called, and I answered their siren call. It seemed as if drug use existed then, but the drug addicts were more refined, dignified, you had to seek them out they hid their addiction, from families and friends. There was heroin use, and alcoholism was rampant in the black community, but it was not as wide open, if you know what I mean. Nevertheless it did not seem to be the problem that it is today. So the bars ruled the neighborhoods, and the heroin users stayed in the background. All the jazz musicians of the day were on heroin, so it seemed like it was not dangerous, as was alcohol. Nevertheless everybody had an alcoholic in their family, or so it seemed. But the black family was in trouble; even then, those who were in charge just did not see what was being sown, and years later, what would be reaped. I was exposed to heroin at an early age, I did not use it but I knew people that did. One of my friends that I grew up with was a heroin addict. His nickname was Johnny Dollar, from the popular song of that era, "Lady, lady, lady, why do you holler, ain't nobody seeing your Johnny Dollar". Now Dollar as we called him let me try some heroin in his house, but I did not like it. I would watch him after he shot up in the bathroom and he would go into this nod where he could not function. I did not want to be like that, beside, it made me sick to my stomach even though I just snorted a little bit of the heroin. Nevertheless Dollar or Calvin as was his real name was a stand up guy, he would ride his bike around like it was his car. He finally got clean from drugs, only to be hit by a car while riding his bike and sustaining a really bad head injury, he was never the same after that accident. Nevertheless heroin addicts did have some style about them, they were for the most part well dressed, not like the crack addicts of now, not like I was, smelly and dirty. A friend of mine who I worked with at Girard Medical Center, Ali, who has been clean for 20 years always, said to me that when they put that crack out, they put shit in the game, the game changed forever, and that is why heroin addicts look down on crack addicts. There may be some truth to that, all of a sudden, the hospitals became overcrowded with crack addicts, the services are even now stretched to the limit by the explosion of crack addicts, and by the neglected children of the crack addicts that are in the human services like Department of Human Services and the insurance companies that pay for the care and hospitalization of these crack addicts have ripped our society apart.

Street Corner Symphony:

Nevertheless, the sixties were alive with music as I mentioned above, music was everywhere in Philadelphia, not just in Detroit with Motown. We had a lot of groups from Philly, with the Intruders, The Stylistics, and Blue Magic. We had the house party, which is where I got my first grind on a girl, her name was Sissy Bray. Of course you could get shot at a house party too, but I went nonetheless. There were these dance clubs and you were not considered important if you did not belong to one. They would wear their club colors and go around and dance against each other, it was a harmless way for guys and girls to compete and win prizes. It was also an alternative to the gangs of that era. We also had the street corner singers in the neighborhood, they would get drunk off of Thunderbird, Tiger Rose or Mad Dog wines, and then they would sing oh so sweet. It was Bunk, Wolf, Barton, Hank Smith, Bobby Linder and my man Bubbles. It was truly a Street Corner Symphony every Friday and Saturday night when there was a lull in the gang wars, or whenever they were drunk, which could be any night. We would sit out on the steps on Toronto Street and listen to the concert, it was something else. They would harmonize, Bubbles would sing bass and bunk would sing falsetto while the rest would sing background vocals. Or they would be at the corner of Carlyle and Clearfield Streets where one of the neighborhood bars were the other being on the corner of 15th and Indiana Avenue. They would sing the songs of the Temptations, the Intruders, the Dells and all of the groups from the sixties. I do believe that they could have been recording artist under different circumstances, if they had not chosen the path that they did, to drink wine all of the time and gang war. Under different circumstances, I guess we all could have been something else, but life is what it is. So they were my introduction to music, as well as I guess my introduction to black men, they were my introduction to hopelessness, to living for the now.

They were my role models, my hero's, they where the ones who I looked up to on the street. I am sure that every neighborhood had someone like them, these men in their late twenties who from the abuse of the streets looked like they were in their forties. They suffered from the abuse of the wine drinking the gang warring, and of course the drug use, using that boy as it was called, that heroin. They intersected my life, intruded on my childhood, introduced me to the streets, yet they were my hero's. I will never forget when I saw Bubbles dunk on an eleven foot basketball court, he was drunk of course and that made it all the more of an amazing thing. Bubbles could not have been more than six feet tall, but that act, the fact that he could dunk even if I did not recognize it for what it was; it was a reminder of what he was before he was an alcoholic. Perhaps he was an athlete before he was a drunk, no matter, he was still a man, but now he was a drunk, mired in self pity. Nevertheless my baby sister Vicky was crazy about him, he would bring her gifts and give her money, very harmless him being in his thirties and her being seven or eight years old. Those street corners, especially 15th and Clearfield Streets were something special, you had the Klein's brothers, Sid and Len, and they had their market there and their laundromat. They were Jewish merchants in the neighborhood; they were the only grocery store that I knew growing up. I remember they had this scam going where they would redeem store coupons and give you a donut for so many coupons, I got many a donut from them, I saved those coupons religiously. Nevertheless, everyone used to hang out at their laundromat, if you were washing clothes or not, and of course someone was always robbing the place, after every weekend you could count on someone robbing that laundromat. It was to the two brothers the price of doing business in the ghetto.

Just Playing Around:

Since we had no playground to play in, we would play on the billboards at 15th and Indiana Avenue, the billboards were very tall. I would guess that they were about three stories tall and where made with a metal frame, like scaffolding that supported them. They would have advertisements on the front of them; they were right by the North Philadelphia train station at Fifteenth Street and Indiana Avenue. But in the back of them you could run and jump from one to the other, but if you fell then that was your ass. All of us, we were so unaware of the danger that we were putting ourselves in, myself and my brothers, Donald, Douglas and Billy, we were just having fun. We were having fun playing games with our neighbors, Dennis, Bernie, Nardie, Craig and Sed and Kevin, just having fun, with Larry and Tommy and Richard. It became the test of your courage as to how far you could jump and how much danger you would be willing to put yourself in. We also played on the railroad spur at 16th and Indiana Avenue at the old Pittsburgh plate glass company that was another very high railroad track about two stories high, it seemed like we had a thing for heights and danger. We would play hide and seek, the one being it would say out loud, "Apple, peach and pumpkin pie, who not ready holler I", then he would try to find each of us before we got back to the base. Also we would play buck-buck, which was a game where you would jump over the person who was bended forward, after you announced yourself by saying" Buck- buck number one coming". The memories of these innocent times fills my heart with joy, the kind of joy that you could never imagine, or perhaps you could, by just recalling the pleasant times of your own childhood. Nevertheless, you think back then that these pleasant times will last forever; you think without knowing any better that these games will go on and stretch into eternity. That you will always be without responsibility, without worries, just wake up everyday with the only concern on your mind is to have a good time within the boundaries of the world which you live in. I never could have imagined the twist and turns that my life would take, back then it just did not seem possible that my life would take the path that it would, but I guess that is the innocence of childhood

We would also play at the train tunnels beneath North Philadelphia train station; the tunnels connected the train stations north and south routes so that you would not have to put yourself in danger by crossing the tracks from one side to another. The tunnels were actually used as an underground fallout shelter during the sixties; they had old food and water stored there and everything else you would need there in case of a nuclear attack. If there was a nuclear attack, we were supposed to run to the tunnels and from there we would be able to survive the radioactive fallout. I also remember the drills that we had in school; you know where we would get underneath our desk in case of a nuclear attack. It was all very stupid now when you look at it, there was no ways that a desk could have protected anyone form a nuclear bomb, or the fallout from an explosion. We would play on the train tracks as if we were born on them; we loved the danger that came with almost getting hit by a train. We would walk up to fifth and Allegheny Avenue to the swimming pool and we would walk the whole way on the train tracks, crazy I guess, but that's just how we were. Once a friend of ours, Tony Miller was burned from the electrical wires that powered the trains, how he survived with just a burn on his leg was nothing short of a miracle. But God looked out for all of us at one time or another. They say that God takes care of the children and the fools; I found that to be true on more than one occasion.

At this time, at the age of fourteen I discovered comic books and my life was never the same. I read everything I could get my hands on, Marvel comics and D. C. comics. I loved Superman and Batman, and of course Spiderman. The Marvel comics were more real to me, the characters seemed more human, The Sub Mariner, Iron Man, Thor and the Hulk, the Fantastic Four and the Avengers. They were my moral compass, from them I learned a sense of right and wrong, they helped to reinforce the values my family taught me. I collected comics and built quite a collection, I began to draw comics and sell them to friends and family. I thought that I would be a comic artist like Jack Kirby who worked for Marvel comics. To me, Jack Kirby was the greatest comic book artist of all time; he had perfected a way to draw a larger volume of work than anyone else did. He drew the Fantastic Four, The Mighty Thor, The Avengers, Iron Man the Incredible Hulk, all in the same month, I thought he was a God.

My friends Larry, Harold and I would go anywhere in our quest to have the best comic collection that three young poor black kids could have, we would even go downtown to the bookstores to steal comics when we had no money. I wonder now how that young child grew and developed into the person that had so many problems, but the comics were both good and bad. Bad in the sense that I hid in this fantasy world, where everyone was equal, in this world, the world of comics, you did not need to socialize with your peers, so my social skills suffered for it. For I never learned at an early age to interact with my own peers, and the social skills necessary to interact with girls, so when the time came for me to do these things, I was unequipped to do so. I guess that you could say that I was a loner, never had a girlfriend when I was growing up, kind of weird I guess, as a matter of fact both Harold and Larry, my comic book buddies never had girlfriends either.

Nevertheless I loved my comics, and they still played an intergal part of my development. My parents recognized this and bought me art sets and I took art lessons. I learned to paint and I even won a painting contest for a Vietnam War theme painting called Make War No More. It was my own fault that I did not pursue this course and become an artist, and later I suffered for it. I remember when I graduated from high school and my parents presented me with an art set, we really could not afford it, but they did it for me nonetheless. I received paints, brushes and an easel, it was wonderful, they tried to give me the opportunity to be an artist, and I just did not follow through.

Despite the objections of my mother and in spite of my upbringing I turned to drugs at an early age, I was about fifteen years old when I had my first drink. And make no mistake about it, alcohol is a drug, just as bad as heroin or crack cocaine, the only difference is that you can buy it from the State Store back then. I got so drunk, my best friend Clayton had to take me to spend the night over his house, I couldn't go home, and my mom would have killed me. Man, my best friend Clayton, he had three sisters that were older than we were, I thought that they were fine, and his mother, Ms. Marie was like a second mother to me, he used to live on fifteen street, then he moved to West Oak Lane, we still kept in touch, we both attended Simon Gratz High school. But he was getting with girls and I was not, so we had to part company when they would have the ditch parties and not go to school, some of those neighborhood girls were having sex even back then. I did not dare miss school though; my father would have killed me.

And that is the basis of this story this journey that I must put down on paper, to not only relieve myself of my burden, but qualify my life and my existence. It started innocently enough, a little peer pressure here, a little wanting to be accepted there and before you know it bam, end of game, at least for a minute, or so it seemed but we will deal with that later. Like I said the drugs gave something to me that was missing in my life, the ability to not be responsible for myself or my actions and because I was always overly responsible, the drugs had to effect me on a sub-conscious level in order for them to work on me. Throughout history all of the people who were overly responsible had to pay the price for being responsible, and most of the times the price they paid was with their lives. This was a burden I was not prepared to carry, or a price I was also not willing to pay. So I ducked, hid from being responsible, like responsibility was someone I didn't want to see. Man self realization is a bitch. So lets continue, like I said it started with the weed, you know a social thing, as if self destruction can be a social thing, but it is in our society. That's one of the first things we learn as a species. Hell do what the other guys are doing, do you want to fit in or not? That's the question we silently ask ourselves on a daily basis whether we know it or not, and we answer it in ways that make us fell comfortable with ourselves. So from smoking weed I graduated to selling weed, man I was so young and I wish I could use ignorance as an excuse, but in reality there was no excuse, for a long time I had a problem excepting responsibility for my own actions.

Am I alone in this? Or is it a normal thing that people do? We have to find some way to justify the pain of our existence, and the suffering of that existence, self justification, that is also a bitch. I guess that if you can justify something, you can justify your actions also, that is how people are able to be cold blooded killers, to them, and the action of murder is justifiable, therefore their actions to them are justified; it is all how you view things I guess. Nevertheless I gravitated between worlds, the right world and the wrong world, with no moral responsibility. How could someone of good and moral upbringing be so easily seduced by the evil of the world that is something I ask myself over and over, with no real answer? It was not as if I didn't have positive role models in my life. My parents and grandparents wanted the best for me, they wanted me to be the first in my family to graduate from college, and they wanted to live their lives through mine. Nothing wrong with that I guess, all parents are in some ways responsible for living through there children. That is what parents do, it is not so much a guilt trip they put us through when we do not live up to their dreams they have for us, they just want the best for us, but to me living up to my parents dreams for me, well that was a lot of responsibility.

2

My High School Years.

When I was growing up, there was a song by War, called slipping into darkness. That song reminds me so much of what was happening in my life at this point. I grew up in the era of house parties, gang war, racial injustice and Motown. This was a time to be alive; the sixties were a jumble of hyperactivity. There were so many things happening in the sixties that it is hard to put it on paper. Like I said earlier, the house parties, man they were happening, for everyone else that is but I, because like I said earlier, was terrified of girls. They just seemed so different. While my friends were enjoying their girl friends, I was concerned with different endeavors. I remember when I was in the 10th grade; a girl who actually thought that I was cute came to my house to claim me. Now she had two of her girlfriends with her, and she scared me to death, as I tried to ignore her and do my homework. Girls were bold back in the day. I remember my first dance with a girl, her name was Debbie, and I got my first slow drag with her. I was very awkward and he just held each other and grinded, I later had a relationship with her, but it did not last long.

I was concerned with helping my family out, so I held a job since I was thirteen years old. I was selling The Evening Bulletin, after school at Cheltenham & Ogontz avenues. I remember my paper route; serve at your own risk. My branch manager was always looking over his shoulder for the 15th and Venango Street gang. These were some terrible dudes, but were just one of many gangs in Philadelphia. These gangs were full of young black men, looking for something, something that they were not getting at home, from school, or from society. So they banded together, like a band of brothers, and gave each other what was missing in their lives. Respect from each other, respect from others, all be it from fear of what they would do to you, but it was respect none the less. And here's the crazy part of the equation, they would put their lives on the line and die for this ideal, for this gang, this street corner. I'm not trying to glorify it, or accept it, just understand it. They called it soldiering. So I learned from an early age to steer clear of those guys, just my brothers gravitated to them. For a few years, they treated me like a stranger, because I chose not to join 15th and Clearfield street gang, now mind you this gang was small potatoes compared to the other gangs out there, but it was something they could call their own. Many a night I can remember the gang getting ready to meet their arch rival at a pre-designated place and time for a rumble. They would ask me, "Are you goanna push it on up with us"? Yeah right, I will be right there I would tell them, and then I would go in the house and watch Star Trek and eat an apple. I loved Star Trek, it debuted on NBC television in 1966 and I thought that it was the coolest thing that I had ever seen; it was a total escape from reality at that time for me. It was created by Gene Roddenberry and it depicted what the future would be like, it was one of the first shows that depicted black people in a positive light, the first being I-Spy with Bill Cosby. It had people of different races, species and religion getting along together and solving problems together.

Man like I said, I was not down with this dying over public property that did not belong to us. Many a night I can remember my mother rushing out the house to gather her sons amid the sounds of gunfire when a rival gang invaded our neighborhood. And you know what? She would come home with them every time. My mother did not play when it came to gang war and being in a gang; she wasn't going to lose a single son to that mess and to that insanity. Nevertheless I learned to take care of myself at an early age, my mom taught me that. And I learned to help out financially by giving my mom some of the money I made from the various odd jobs I kept. But there were good times with my dad too. He was our Boy Scout leader, and he tried to instill in us the things he learned in the army, like responsibility, but we were just boys. Nevertheless my dad did take us on some overnight camping trips. I remember we once went to a Boy Scout Jamboree that was held in Fairmount Park. A jamboree is where scouts from all over the world come together at a preordained place for a weekend of good time's good memories, and good vibrations. My scout troop even won a gold medal in the 4x4 relay; it felt so good to get those medals at the award ceremony. That whole weekend was one of the best times of my life; we met Boy Scouts from England, from India, from France and all over the world. During the day we would watch wild eagles fly above us, and during the night we would lie on our backs and watch shooting stars, it was the best.

My mom was a Cub Scout pack leader, they both were concerned with other people, and that's what I learned from them, is to be concerned about other people. Once my father took us on a day hike, we had full packs on. It was December and it was snowing outside, we marched through Fairmount Park, to West Philadelphia, from 17th and Allegheny Avenue to 52nd and Parkside Avenue. It was so cold, that my feet were freezing by the time that we arrived there. Once we got to West Philly and we had to build a fire, the march was so that we could qualify and earn our winter merit badges. So we built the fire, we put cans of Campbell soup directly into the fire, and we made hot tea to drink, it was miserable and it kept right on snowing. We took the cans of soup out of the fire before they exploded and opened them up, even with the hot tea, the hot soup and the fire, I could not get warm and none of us could. Then we had to march back through the park to North Philly. I could not wait to get home and get warm, we had many such experiences in the Boy Scouts, and it was and remains an amazing experience in my life that I will never forget.

Learning Humanity from My Parents:

The ability to give was like I said a gift I learned from my family, like the time they took in a homeless friend of ours, his name was Tony. Everybody in the neighborhood always made fun of him because he was dirty all the time, he smelled, and had nowhere to live. So my parents got him, gave him a bath, fed him and he lived with us for a while. Now this was at a time when we did not have enough room or food for ourselves, but to this day when I see him, he always asks about my mom and dad, their intervention saved his life. So from my parents, my grandparents I learned the valuable lesson of self sacrifice and giving of you to others. Also the seeds of spirituality were planted at an early age; both my grandparents lived in the church. This was a time when the black church meant something in the black community. The civil rights movement that I was privileged to see and experience was a movement that could not have went forth without the strength and spiritual guidance of the church. The Southern Christian Leadership Council was responsible for most of the advances we as black people have made, and many of the freedoms that we enjoy. Through the self sacrifice of the N.A.A.C.P. and its members we now can vote, go to college and hold jobs that were once denied us. We cannot forget that people gave their lives for this, that they made the ultimate sacrifice. Now the black church is a lion without any teeth in the black community. It has been sold out like other religions, ripped off like jazz, ripped of like the Indians, ripped off like nature. We are being ripped off. The black church has morphed into this commercial enterprise that benefits those in power. It has become a sad commentary as to where we are as a people and as a race.

So like I was saying my childhood was hard, and I learned a lot of lessons from it. The only mistake I really made was not applying those lessons to my life, but it is never too late. I attended Simon Gratz High school; this was in an era where you really risked your life in pursuit of an education because you could be killed trying to go to school because you had to pass through a rival gang's territory. Nevertheless I was also saved by going to school. I was placed in an accelerated program that academically attempted to keep young black students focused, so that made me a geek I guess, and the gang members saw no advantage to beating up a geek. But I still bared witness to the savagery of my times, sometimes a silent witness as I attempted to blend into the background and not be noticed or responsible, I had to do that just to live another day. I was given summer jobs through the Prodigy program when I was in high school; this was when I was seventeen years old. The Prodigy

Program was the brain child of Dr. Marcus Foster, who was the superintendent of Philadelphia public schools at the time. Dr Foster later left Philadelphia to take the same post in Oakland California as the superintendent of their public schools. He was shortly thereafter assassinated by the Simbianese Liberation Army. It was really a sad commentary to the state of America at that time. The government had taught us that if you do not like someone, kill him or her. The sixties have to be considered the decade of the assasination. People think that it started with President John F. Kennedy, but his was merely the most famous murder. You could literally get away with murder; it was just too many people getting killed in the sixties. With the war in Vietnam, the assassinations back at home; it was as if the world was about to self imploded, it was a very dangerous time. It was a tragic waste for Dr. Marcus Foster was a true educator, and deeply cared about children and education.

So the Prodigy program exposed me to jobs in the field of science which was my field of choice. One job I worked at was at Moss Rehabilitation Hospital. The government was funding a program there; they were trying to find a cure for nerve gas. So they built this isolation chamber right in the hospital on the top floor. It was a surreal place apart from the rest of the hospital, yet it was there. They had this big mainframe computer a Sperry with a sit in console. This was before personal computers; they were still on the drawing board. And computers used magnetic tape to store information; the floppy disk would come later. So anyway, this government sponsored program needed subjects, and they used patients, without the consent of the patients or the family. They made sure all the patients that they used for subjects in the experiments were stroke victims who could not speak, they were there for rehabilitation. Nevertheless they placed them in the isolation chamber, and injected them with a drug called atropine; we then watched the effects the drug had on them. They had some sort of biofeedback device hooked up to the patients, and the computer registered the results. To watch those elderly people and their response to the drug was something else. Sometimes it appeared they were on some kind of LSD trip, and for hours they would be forced to sit there strapped in the chair against their wills. When their families came to visit, you could see the patients trying to communicate what they were going through to their family members, but their speech centers no longer worked, and they could not speak. Most of the patients there were recovering from strokes, so I guess that's why they were used because many had slurred speech and could not talk clearly.

The government will do so anything it has to do to achieve its means, those elderly people that we used for these experiments were looked at as collateral damage. Now that I look back on this experience I know it was wrong, but at the time I was a fifteen year old kid, and besides they were giving me a paycheck. That was probably the first time I sold out my values, it was the first time I looked the other way because my palm was being greased. Fantastic! I had no idea at the time, but my morals were being compromised and that society was preparing me for the path that I chose to take later on.

My next year in the Prodigy Program we were making a film about the Prodigy Program. The film would be presented to the government and the programs funding would be renewed. We worked out of Temple Universities Instructional Communication Department. They operated solely to produce instructional films for the Temple University medical school, and while there I got to work with a guy who was a cameraman for the Captain Noah show, his name was Malachi Hogan. Captain Noah was a children's show that I watched growing up, so working with him was a thrill. We got to help with the filming of some instructional films. One such film was that of an autopsy. Now we had just come back from lunch, and were told to get the equipment, so we grabbed the cameras, lights and so forth. We went to the old medical building at Broad and Tioga Streets and once there we were taken to this room by a doctor. The room contained a long table like the kind in an operating room. On the table was a long bag, a body bag. Like the ones you see on television, or in war movies, only at the time I didn't know what it was. So the doctor comes back in, and removes the body from the bag, and this old white guy looked like he was on the high side of 100 years, perfectly preserved, a little guy. And the doctor proceeded to cut into this guy's chest, showing the different layers of the skin. Of course all our lunches came up, so much for Mickey-Dees.

Nevertheless the experience was helpful in my life because it broadened my horizons, and exposed me to things that I would not have ordinarily been exposed to. So I am thankful for that because just as I was exposed to science, the real world still beckoned to me and sometimes I answered. I remember one time I was working at Gino's. Does anybody remember them? They were here before McDonalds, as a matter of fact, they were to my generation what McDonalds is to this generation. Man, they introduced Kentucky Fried Chicken to the world, and the Gino's Giant; well anyway I worked there after school until closing which means I was there very late. And looking back on this, God must have been looking out for me, as he still does today, because I was out here pretty late every night, and was not killed, like so many other young black men. So this one particular night, we were closing the store, it was located at American and Lehigh Avenue it was a pretty desolate area, so these two rival gangs had decided to meet there for a gang war. Now here I am watching this through the big plate glass window, like it was a one hundred and fifty inch plasma television. The gang members were so intent on what they were doing that they never even noticed us in the store. The gang members had zip guns, and car antennas, and knives. It was like a scene out of the movie Gangs of New York. It sure looked like it had been staged by Martin Scorsese. For its brutishness and sheer violence, to this day I can say that I have never witnessed anything like it. It was like some sort of Roman gladiator spectacle. I mean each gang was an individual army, hundreds of guys clashing into each other, it was surreal. The only reality of it was when the sirens started to get closer and closer, which forced the gangs to disband, they even took their wounded with them like a modern day army. I mean they had logistics, support, generals and enlisted men. Nevertheless, by the time I got finished work which was a short time later and as I waited for the bus, it was as if nothing had ever happened. I believe to this day that if the police had never come, those guys would still be fighting, all these decades later, that's how strong their misguided hate for each other was.

3

Growing up in the Seventies.

At that point in my life I had had enough of school having just completed twelve years of it. I was seventeen years old and I really wanted to be an artist, but my guidance councilor in high school fucked that up, and I winded up missing the SAT's. So I tried going to Penn. State and again the wrong information led my dad to drive all the way to State College Pennsylvania only to be told that the SAT's were important. So I took the SAT's. At that point a series of events went to into place, almost like divine intervention that put me on the right path in spite of myself. My mother became very ill; I passed my SAT's, and was accepted to go to Lincoln University. I did so to help make her better, and I knew that was my only chance to amount to something, so I took it. I remember visiting my mother in the hospital right after her surgery with my acceptance letter in my hand, it gave her the will to live, she was so proud of me. My mother got better, and all was well so it seemed. Nevertheless, life is not what is all cracked up to be, I went to Lincoln more concerned with getting high and fitting in than I did with my studies. I had the ability to do well in college, but I set myself up to fail, almost as if it was a self fulfilling destiny, to this day I have not figured it out.

My College Years at Lincoln University:

Nevertheless I would pay the price later for my transgression because to me college life was one big party, drinking smoking weed, and the only thing I missed out on was the women. Even though I was not a bad looking guy, man girls frightened the heck out of me. I grew up in a large family. I had nine brothers and sisters. My parents were both only children, so I supposed that's why they had such a large family. I can remember that during such great time of wealth for this country my mother struggled to feed us. There were times when the food ran out; this was the times of surplus government handouts. But there was more, a shadow on my life and my family's life; it was this thing that could not be explained away. This thing that was not talked about, this separate but unequal status that I can even to this day remember and the stain it left on me socially, psychologically and spiritually. Oh sure I can remember going to church at a young age, so I was exposed to religion and belief in God, but it just didn't take, but the seeds were planted to be harvested at a later date. I was taught the basic principles of right and wrong, and these principals saved me later in life as you will discover as my story unveils itself to you. But there still existed emptiness, a spiritual void that this society marked me with as it marked all people that were different from the dominant culture. Preparation to fail, that's what my life was about, and learning not to take responsibility for my actions was a big part of my development.

Rizzo's Police:

This life I was prepared to lead was flawed, but that was the plan for me. That was my manifest destiny, and I followed it and played it to the hilt. So in college I gravitated to the wrong things, the wrong choices, and did not finish for various reasons. Money, lack of financial aid and also lack of effort and let's not forget that. Nevertheless while in college an event took place that really for tested my belief in people both white and black, I was nineteen years old, it was 1973. It happened between my sophomore and junior years at Lincoln University. We had just been let out for summer vacation, and I was you know enjoying a little down time before I looked for a summer job. I had to work every summer to earn money for the things I needed for school like books, a new stereo and some new clothes. I remember I got up late, took a bath and was in my parent's bedroom getting some lotion, when I could see the flashing of police light on the walls of the bedroom. So I look out the window and I see my brothers fighting two police officers. I still had on just my shorts and bedroom slippers and by the time I got down the stairs, the block was full of police officers and all of the neighbors were out of their houses, now remind you we grew up on a small narrow one way street. This was of course during the times of the dreaded Frank Rizzo; he was the Philadelphia police commissioner. During this time the Philadelphia police was mostly white and they had a license to kick a nigger's ass. So it was insanity, I just did not know how insane it was, as I approached one of the police officers to ask what was going on, he responded "He's one of them grab him". So they grabbed me and threw me in the back of the police wagon with my three younger brothers. My three brothers ranged in age from sixteen years old to fourteen years old. Try to imagine yourself at fourteen years old being called racist names. Being disrespected and treated like an animal, and what that must do to a young developing mind and psyche. They called every name in the book including 'black fucking niggers". The situation was about to become a riot as my neighbors and friends tried to intervene on our behalf. Someone went and got my grandmother Mom-mom; who lived around the corner from us. This lady whom I respected so much, so strong in the church and her faith in God and this still makes so fucking mad to recount this, well she was called a "black bitch" and a "fucking nigger". She was totally disrespected by the white police officers as we were held in the back of the police wagon like caged animals. She began to weep, and I'm watching all this from the police van window. So they finally fight their way through the crowd and the police van pulls off with us in it. Now there is an unnatural silence as take stock of my brother's condition. William is bleeding profusely from the middle of his face thanks to a big 6 ft 5in 300 pound officer who just beat the shit out of him, my other two brothers Douglas and Donald are also nicked up. So never having been exposed to this type of violence or activity, I naively ask no one in particular, what are they going to do to us know? My youngest brother Donald replies, they're going to take us to the police station and kick our asses.

I couldn't accept that answer, one because he was only fourteen years old and what did he know plus "We've got rights" I proudly said.

This is America"; they can't do that to us, as I said that my brothers Donald and William both laughed as if I was telling a joke or something, I would learn that they knew better than I did. As I said that the van pulled into the back of the 39th police district at 22nd and Huntington Park Avenue. There was silence, and then there were voices laughing, talking and planning. Then the doors of the van suddenly swung open. It must have been shift change because they had every cop in the division lined up on both side of the van, and they were all white, and they had an assortment of weapons, blackjacks, nightsticks you name it they had it. Then they began to call us every name in the book, "Come on out you black fucking niggers they shouted". You wanted to fight before well come on out and fight now you black mother fuckers. The police officers outside of the patrol wagon shouted this over and over. With that my brother Douglas jumped from the truck. As he ran they immediately begin to chase him and beat him. As I stepped down from the back of the wagon I was swarmed by an untold number of cops and one took his knight stick and cracked the top of my left foot. It was as if time stopped for a minute, and as I looked down at my foot began to swell, almost as if it were in slow motion until the skin burst and it began to bleed. This surreal scene and the silence were broken by my Brother William's screams. I turned to see that same big cop taking his frustrations out on William as if it was a grudge match, with blood spurting from William's face as the cop swung and hit him over and over again. We were placed in a holding cell, my brothers William and Douglas were bleeding so bad that they had to take them to the hospital. My brother Douglas had a big gash in his head because when he ran form the police wagon they caught him and beat him in the head. My foot hurt so bad where they had split it open that I needed to go but I was not about to leave my brother Donald alone so I stayed with him at the police district. I do not know if many people have had the opportunity to be arrested, but while in the cell there is a natural chatter of activity that you can overhear outside of the cell. You can hear the police officers as they make jokes about what they had just done, it almost sounds natural, but hearing other human beings laughing about hurting another human being well there is nothing natural about that.

Even the captain of the police district asked what happened to them as they were taking my two brothers to the hospital. Now I thought this man will intervene, he is in charge and he can not possibly condone this kind of inhuman behavior. Well the other cop replied "They bumped their heads in the wagon", and they all began to laugh and as they laughed my hopes for justice sank even lower. At that point I realized to them that we were not human, and they treated us accordingly. As the silence came over the cell, the sadness that I had experienced all my life overtook me. Sure I was young enough to remember Jim Crow, but to experience it like this, man what a shock it was to me to realize that maybe you are second class, maybe you are worthless. We were quickly moved, because my family by had now assembled to address what had happened to us. So the cops took us from one police station to another, one step ahead of my family. At one point as we were being moved from the 39th district three cops escorted me handcuffed. Two were very huge guys, one was at the police limit for being short in height whatever that was at the time he was maybe five feet five inches. He took this opportunity to let me know that he was in charge He asked me what happened as if he was really concerned about me as we walked toward the van, so I related the situation to him.

He then became very angry when I finished my story and he said, "Don't you know when the cops come you run nigger", and he proceeded to hit me with all his might in my stomach which was exposed because I was handcuffed with my hands behind me. This white cop hit me with everything that he had; he hit me with all the raw naked hatred that he could muster. He hit me with all the racial hate that he could generate; the hatred came from somewhere deep inside of him and exploded into my body from his, like the transfer of some sort of power. Nevertheless to my surprise, it did not hurt that much, at least not as much as I expected it to. Perhaps it was the adrenalin that was pumping through my body, or perhaps it was because my fear and hatred protected me in some way. Then the other to cops shoved me as hard as they could, I stumbled and almost fell but regained my balance when I heard my late brother Donald yell from the police van "Don't fall down or they will beat you up again". By that time they had bought Douglas and William back from the hospital, they were bandaged up and still bloody, and then they proceeded to get us out of the district because my parents had called to see if we were there. My father, outraged was arrested for coming to the police station with a gun. My mother, grandmother and grandfather finally caught up with us at the Broad & Champlost Streets police station. Even though it was summer I remember being very cold in those holding cells. My grandfather took his shirt off and gave it to me when they were finally allowed to see us, for I had no shirt on. They knew that we were at the 39th police district because my mother found one of my bedroom slippers there. My mother was very calm even though she was crying; she assured me that everything would be alright. I wondered what she meant, and soon found out she was told that since I was nineteen years old and that I would have be sent to the Roundhouse and arrested, while my brothers who were minors at the time would be released to her. Thus was the beginning of my criminal record, and at the tender age of nineteen I was exposed to the seedy world of the criminal.

I was told once that the establishment needed all black males to have criminal records, for tracking purposes, like they put radio collars on wild animals, so they can tell what you are doing and where you are at all times. I was suddenly afraid, scared and alone as they took me alone back to the cell and released my three brothers. It was growing dark outside even though it was summer which told me it was about 9 p.m. I was placed in the back of a police van to begin my journey to a place I could never imagine existed until now. I began to feel that I hated white people; I hated all whites for the pain I was feeling physically and emotionally. My foot was aching, my whole body was numb with fear, and this was the plan for the black man I thought. To be cataloged, fingerprinted so I could be tracked like an animal in some insidious research experiment, Wild Kingdom, bought to you by Mutual of Omaha. As we arrived, this place was like an unreal surreal kingdom all its own. With its own laws, own code and own judge, guilty until proven innocent. Here the wheels of justice ground to a halt. Here I was a nineteen year old kid, thrust into a place I was unprepared for. It was the bowels of the earth, with all those considered to deviant to be a part of normal society; little did I dream that it was a place I would see again before my life's journey was over. It was populated with drunks, dope fiends, drug pusher, prostitutes, transvestites, murderers, you name it they had it. One white guy was so beat up and swollen from his beating that you could not even see his eyes, he was there for killing someone with his car in a traffic accident. The sad thing is that he was so drunk when it happened that he could not remember what happened as he sobered up. He kept repeating that the cops said I killed somebody with my car, he had a nice suit on, and not that even mattered anymore. He was now reduced to being a well dressed criminal. Nevertheless the police who were so overwhelmed became insensitive to all the human pain, suffering and the degradation going on around them. The next lesson I learned is that they control you with hunger; the cops only fed prisoners in the holding tank, the Bubble it was called, every twelve hours.

They gave you a cheese sandwich; I'm talking one slice of cheese between to slices of bread and eight ounces of juice. Here in the Bubble there was no social class, which was strange; there were the rich with the poor, the violent offender with the non-violent offender, and the White man with the Black man and Hispanic man. It seemed crime had no color or class; everyone was the same in the eyes of the turnkey it was quite an awaking for me. The turnkey was the police officer that controlled everything because he had the key to the door of the Bubble, he controlled when you went to the bathroom, now that is a lot of power, the power to decide who goes to the bathroom and who does not. The other thing that I remembered from that experience was that I could not get comfortable, no one could, the benches were made of wood and very narrow, there was not enough room for everyone in the Bubble, so the alpha males got the best seats. You know the most violent and biggest guys the most comfortable positions, the rest of us had to lay under the benches, wherever we could. Then there were the guys on the one phone in the Bubble, calling their girlfriends to come bail them out, cursing them and calling them bitches when they could not come down to the Roundhouse, everybody lined up to use the phone there, the cost of a call which was a quarter which was golden if you had any change. So there I sat waiting to go before the judge, watching this human tragedy play out before my eyes. The seconds turning into minutes and the minutes turning into hours, tick tock, tick tock, until finally my name was called. You are led from the Bubble to the courtroom upstairs shackled together like animals, easier to control by only two cops.

Now what happened next blew my mind, behind the glass panel, where the families sit at in the gallery, was all of my family and I mean everyone and they determined not to leave without me, I had never felt as loved as I did this night. And they were all there, my mother, my father, Nana, Ruthie, Aunt Marion. So I went home after the judge set bail for me, I was forever scarred and would never be the same again; for the real world had exploded upon me and embraced me with all its violent fury. The ugliness of the society that my mother and father attempted to shield me from had reared its ugly head and shown me what it was to be black in America in the nineteen seventies. Nevertheless what happened next was crazier even still, in order to protect themselves and to justify the violence that they perpetrated against me and my brothers, the Philadelphia police department concocted a story and a lie. The police claimed that they saw my brother exiting from a locked neighborhood candy store, which was a lie. I had to travel back and forth from Lincoln University to my trial as I was being tried for burglary. The person who owned the store was a friend of the family and testified that my brothers worked in the store and the charges were dropped. My mother filed a complaint with the American Civil Liberties Union, and we then sued the City Of Philadelphia. We could not afford a lawyer so this lawyer handled our lawsuit pro-bono, we won our case, but after the lawyer got his money, I only got $300.00 dollars, my brothers got $600.00 dollars apiece, all of that pain and suffering for a lousy $300.00 dollars, it did not seem right, but that is the way it was.

Gang Wars:

Oh I had seen violence before; remember this was the era of the most violent self perpetrated genocide that even rivals what black's people are doing to themselves now. The gang wars of the late sixties and early seventies exacted a devastating toll, as some 400 plus young men were killed each year over street corners that didn't even belong to them. I could never understand the allure of dying for something as trivial as a street corner, but hundreds of young black men willing did so. I remember when a friend of mine was killed. We played basketball together, and we went swimming together, and we were in the Boy Scouts together. Then one summer night he was killed. We were told the next day, it was a surreal atmosphere. He was there one day and gone the next. He was sixteen years old. His name was Richard Harrell, I remember first his smile and his laughter, his joke playing and his humanity, you really miss those things about a person, one killed so young. The times we went swimming, the adventures we all shred growing up, the stripping away of the innocence of childhood, that's what I remember the most. Richard's family handled it well I guess, although I could tell that they were hurting, they had a large family like mines, 10 children, and then just like that one was gone. At that point, we were no longer children that had been stripped away from us. So his family was left to carry on, and like my brothers Richard dabbled in gang membership, but like my brothers it was a membership driven by the need to belong to something and from that belonging to feel protected from Venango Street. Those of us who lived in the neighborhood were forced to handle it in another way, almost like he was killed in Vietnam, a casualty of war. Yeah there was a lot of violence in the sixties and seventies, even the girls got into it. A female friend of mine was killed one Saturday night at a party, just down the street from her home. I was sixteen at the time, and she was too. She was a beautiful girl named Linda Roundtree. She was stabbed by a mutual friend a girl that we both went to elementary school with named Victoria. They say that Victoria belonged to the 17th and Venango Street gang, and that Linda was with the 25th and Westmoreland Streets gang, but I never believed that. Victoria had a troubled life, she wore a wig in elementary school, and on the last day of school, a friend of mine named Andre decided he was going to run by and snatch the wig off of her head, he did and a fight ensued and she beat the shit out of him. Kids always made fun of her because of her weight, and lack of hair; she served ten years in prison for the murder of Linda, a waste of two lives, the story of the street. Gang violence affected every facet of black life during that time, and to a very negative extent. Many young people answered the call with devastating effects on them and their families.

The violence of the sixties exploded into the seventies like an avalanche, with devastating effects on the black community. The childhood that was lost was to become the childhood of violence, where people would be here one day and dead the next, the victim of gang violence. I remember Wolf, from the 25th and Westmoreland Street gang, he would sit in the laundromat at 15th and Clearfield Street, and watch us as we went to school, I liked him a lot. I never sure how deep his affiliation with the gangs was, but then one day the police found him on the railroad tracks, brutally beaten and stabbed to death. I remember it so well because he was the first person that I knew that would be killed by gang violence, even before Richard was. His younger sister who worshiped the ground that he walked on and his family was devastated by his death, as was our community; little did we know that this was only the beginning. It was almost as if no one cared that young black men were dying at an enormous rate. I remember one time when 15th and Venango streets came down to fight my neighborhood and Barton who lived around my neighborhood was from the 25th and Westmoreland streets gang came running down Toronto Street chasing Venango Street back toward 15th and Toronto Streets, he was so drunk that he fired a shotgun into the trees on 15th street. He really killed that tree as the leaves came falling down; it would have been funny if it was not so pathetic and scary. I watched this from the doorway of my house on Toronto Street, staying in the shadows, hoping not to be spotted, least I become a victim of the violence. My next door neighbor Steven was sentenced to life imprisonment for his part in a gang related murder, he is still incarcerated 35 years later, and Steven will never see the light of day again.

Another time I came home from school, and my mother's best friend from across the street, Mrs. Elsie, was in our kitchen crying. Her son along with another young man had been found in a house around the corner; both of their throats had been slit. They were both tied up and gagged. It appears they had this scam where they would sell this gun over and over to different people, then take the gun back and sell it to someone else. This was the way that they supported their heroin addictions, I geuss it caught up with them. I really liked Hank, which was his name. His friend who was killed with him I did not care for, his name was Terry, and he always tormented me for some reason that I could not understand, he was older and was able to get away with it. With the race riots, the war in Vietnam, assassinations of our leaders, it appeared no one was safe. It seems to me that those who were in charge were preparing the way for what is going on now. As if all that violence was needed to shape the world we live in. Like certain groups were indeed enacting some grim Manifest Destiny bullshit. Man it was crazy, but what happened afterward was crazier even still.

We have lost something, once we were at our best when things were at there worst, this has been documented many times. The civil rights movement was but one example, but we as human beings are also capable of unspeakable atrocities against each other as Hitler for one proved. By the time the criminal justice system had ran it's course, I was now twenty years old, I went back to Lincoln University, and as I said did not finish, but learned some more valuable lessons about life. In my last year there, I was awarded a co-op job, which is a program to expose student to various fields, I was twenty years old. I was sent to work in Washington D.C. I was a science major so I went to work for a laboratory that did government testing and research. It was called The Insitute for Behavioral Research. They did a lot of useless experiments on primates and other infra-human subjects, like rats and other things. Now there's an interesting word, "infra-human", something not determined to be human by the dominant culture or the dominant race, sound familiar?

People Are Good And People Are Bad:

Nevertheless, while working there something happened that changed my life and my view of humanity, just as the incident with the Philadelphia police had changed me and filled with venom for ever white person, I was given a chance to reapraise these feelings. You see God has this plan for all of us, and always knows where he wants us to be, it's up to us to follow the path, to pay attention and to listen and to learn. Sometimes the background noise in our lives is so loud that we can not hear what God is saying to us, but this one time it all fell into place. I was alone in a new city, I had a few friends from Lincoln University who lived in Washington, but for the most part this was a new experience for me. The school found me a place to live. It was in a boarding house in North West Washington near 14th and Otis Place. Now this was also the first time I was exposed to mental illness in a very personal way, sure that mentally ill old man had tricked me and friends with the bike thing years ago, but this was different. One of the other tenents suffered from what I now know was schizophrenia, she talked to herself day and night and she would never come out of her room, and I thought it was two separate people in the room, so I was pretty afraid of that.

Then I had to learn my way to work, I worked in Silver Spring, Maryland. Nevertheless while I was working there in Silver Spring Maryland, I met a co-worker named Pete, I can't even remember his last name. It seems like a life time ago. Well Pete he took me under his wing, he made sure that I learned my way around, just really showed me humanity and kindness, and oh by the way did I mention that Pete was a white person? Nevertheless that played in intergal part to this story because while he was doing this for me, he also seemed to be missing a lot of work, and his co-workers said nothing about it, like no one wanted to mention it. You know how a group of people get together and no one talks about a certain subject because it might be taboo, well that's how it was. I later learned why nobody talked about it, you see Pete's wife was dying of cancer, and he spent every moment visiting her at the hospital, taking care of his children, and working and of course looking after some inner-city black kid who didn't know his way around Silver Spring and Washington D.C. When I found out about Pete's circumstances that really blew me away because now I was forced to deal with that hatred for white people that I had carefully crafted, nurtured and carried around for so long That hatred had become an intergal part of who I was, any failure in blacks, and any failure of mines, I before this incident with Pete could blame on the white man, that racist motherfucker that was keeping me down. Now I was suddenly stripped of that racial bias, that crutch that I had been leaning on like a cripple. I realized that it wasn't all white people that beat me and my brothers; it was that white policeman that beat us that day. Now I had to step back and take stock of who I was and what I thought about white people, that is what my interactions with Pete forced me to do and that was a precious gift that he gave to me. Pete taught me to once again to look at people as people, to look at and judge them by who they are, and not by the color of their skin to judge each individual on an individual basis. He gave back my humanity, and that is something I will always be grateful for, thanks Pete.

But that was one shinning moment; another was the discovery of how much my parents loved me, especially my mom. You see one day we were chasing monkeys in the primate room; the doctors needed one for an experiment. The monkey ran under the cages, now you have to be very careful with the monkeys because for anyone who does not know it they have very sharp canine teeth, much likes a dog. So I and this student from the University of Maryland, who was working there for the summer also, we had to catch the monkey and as I stood up I banged the top of my head into the metal door, because I was in a squatting position. I was knocked unconscious and I woke up in the lab with a splitting headache. I went home and the pain got worser and worser, and I could not sleep that night. I got up the next day and went to work and fell out. I woke up in the emergency room at a nearby hospital, and Pete was there. He called my mother and assured her I was alright. I was diagnosed with a severe concussion, given some medication, and sent home after several hours of observation. Nevertheless what happened next was a shock even to me. My mom got on a bus and came immediately to Washington D.C., from Philadelphia. She stayed with me all that day to make sure I was alright, fixed me something to eat, and caught the last bus back to Philly that night. My mother and I always shared a special bond, and it was proven that day. Also my dad came up the next Saturday to see me. We went to dinner, went to see One Flew over the Cuckoo's Nest, and afterward he went back home. Both of theses incidents really blew my mind, and I have good memories and am thankful to both of them for the concern and love that they showed me during that day.

Act Two:
Slipping Into Darkness.

4

Planting the Seeds for Failure in College.

Yet all this time, I was as a person developing character flaws that would haunt me and shape me for the rest of my life. I grew up thinking that drugs and the drug culture was in fact the dominant culture. Hell everyone I knew was using or selling drugs, and my parents' generation, and my grandparent's generation knew nothing about this counter-culture, or preferred not to know about it. It was the late sixties and the hippie movement was in full swing. The war in Vietnam had divided the country and as I said earlier, the sixties were the decade of assignation. We as black people, after having been focused so well on the civil rights movement, began to lose our way, and our focus. It seemed to me that once we became assimilated into the dominant culture through the courts that black people lost there cohesiveness. The very things that made us great as a people was taken away, as we now were caught up in the race to keep up with the Jones. We stopped educating ourselves, our traditional black colleges began to fall on hard times and we became like the culture that we lived in. We stopped caring about each other and began to care only about money and that is really what this country is about. Greed is good, the acquisition of personal wealth any cost, whether it be at the cost of another human being, or another family it no longer mattered. So we learned to play the game of America, and we were swallowed up like everything else that America swallows up, can you say Native American?

I started to use drugs in high school, mostly drinking, then I was introduced to pot, my brothers were selling it and knew a guy who had connections. So when I went away to school, I started to sell it up there too. My time at Lincoln University was my first experience away from home. Being a black school of course too much attention was paid to partying and looking good. Although some people were able to get a good education, but you had to really work at it, most of us were there for the wrong reasons. We played basketball high, we went to class high, hell we even sat in class and smoked pot, with the teacher giving a lecture. It was in one of those really big lecture halls, like an auditorium, and we sat way in the back at the top because it had like stadium seating. We decided to smoke some weed in a tobacco pipe, and to cover the smell, my friend mixed in some tobacco. Well me not being a cigarette smoker, it made me violently ill, I had to leave class and go lay down. Another bad experience with drugs was that my freshman year, we were going to have a concert with Earth Wind and Fire. I got so drunk passed out in my friend George's and Ricky's dorm room, and I woke up the next day to find that I had missed everything. These stories not withstanding, I was emotionally unprepared for college, and my interpersonal skills were underdeveloped. And of course I could not relate to girls my own age. And I had some fine girls after me, I just couldn't close the deal, everyone else was getting laid but not me, I missed out on a lot of sex because of that. Nevertheless I still went on panty raids with my friends, and began to grow, not as a scholar, but as a druggie.

I began to be introduced to and take a wide range of drugs there was acid, hallucinating drugs like mushrooms, peyote buttons, mescaline and THC. Nevertheless reefer had exotic names like Panama Red, Acapulco Gold and Columbian Brown. There were the Thai-sticks from Thailand and man we had it all, and used it all it was one big party. The outside world did not exisit to us, the world of our parents and their rules did not exisit to us, we made up our own world, and in this deviant world we made our own rules. I was fortunate enough to have a program on the local college radio station, W.L.I.U. was the call letters, and I was on every Saturday night, from six p.m. until ten p.m. I was lucky enough to meet some good people through the radio program. Now, my friend Tino, or George he was also a dick jockey on W.L.I.U. and he was able to leverage that into much sex, he got it coming and going, even my other friend from high school Richard was able to get some, me; well it was just passing me by. I remember one incident that still haunts me, there was a girl, Denise, she was as untouchable as could be, and she was from Pittsburgh Pennsylvania. Denise was a cheerleader, now imagine, me with a cheerleader, a guy like me with a cheerleader, anyway she invited me to her dorm room one evening, it was rumored that she was sleeping with the basketball coach. Her cheerleading routine was as dramatic as it got, she would do this split that was unbelievable. Well she invites me over, she had no roommate for that semester, she had just got out of the shower and she had on her underwear and a robe. We sat and talked for a while, me very nervous, and her waiting for me to make a move on her; she was very much a lady. I just did not know what to do, so we sat there until she got tired of my incompetence and asked me to leave; I still have dreams about her, what would have happened if we had made love. Man, she was so hot, I would go to her home city to find her if I knew where she was. Then there was homecoming each year. Being the first black college in America had its advantages. We were able to get the hottest acts of the day. I'm talking the New Birth, Kool & Gang, The K-Gees, Rufus featuring Chaka Chan, The BT-Express, we had them all. By that time my brother Douglas was also attending Lincoln University, so we were able to invite my best friend Clayton to the concerts, and he was able to bring my younger brothers William and Donald since he was driving. He had a Volkswagen Carmen Gia, man that car got around. At the Kool & Gang show, I remember my brothers coming to get me as Clayton fell out in the concert; he was drinking without having anything on his stomach so he got sick we had to take him back to my dorm room, and I missed most of the concert.

These were some good times, but there was something wrong, my drug use got worse. As my friends from Philly were going to class, we all majored in psychology, I, George and Richard. They continued to strive toward their degrees, and I just lost all hope and did not take advantage of the opportunity that was presented to me, a college diploma. I mean George and Richard did a lot of partying too, as well as Bob Felton and Ashley, even Billy Jones, but they stayed on task and graduated, I did not. There was the party in the student union building that George and Richard threw for their fraternity, Solid Phi Solid, I provided the music and I blew out my Pioneer speakers, I still have that picture form the party, me with this wild flowered shirt on and George, both of us with our afros. I remember at one concert, I and my friend Billy took some acid and we sat so high in the bleachers that I thought we were going to fly away. That reminds me of my friend Billy Jones. We smoked a lot of reefer together, and sold much more than we smoked. He would take acid, and his trip was to sit in the room and listen to all the Jimmy Hendrix albums in chronological order by year, he was afraid to leave the room, while I wanted to be around other people, so I would go to the girls' dormitory, that acid affected everybody differently. One year Billy let me sleep in his dormitory room, on the floor for an entire semester because my financial aid did not come through. Billy wanted to be a boxer so he began to train with Ashley; they used to put each other through the ringer with their sparring sessions. And my friend Bob Felton, he had this cool collection of boxing films, we would watch all of these great fights from the twenties, the thirties and up to modern times, I really learned to appreciate Ali from those films. I remember that we were all in the dormitory room in January of 1974 when Ali lost to Ken Norton. There was silence throughout the entire campus, you would have thought that someone had died; it was close to that because our hero had been defeated. Muhammad Ali for us had transcended sports; he was to black people a national hero, someone to look up to. Everyone knows the story of how he gave up the heavyweight championship of the world because of his principals and beliefs and his not wanting to be inducted into the service during the Vietnam War. Ali was our hero, he came from poverty to become champion, he fought for his religious beliefs and he was a Muslim when it was very unpopular to be one. So when he lost, it seemed like we all lost, to us Ken Norton became the oppressor, Ken Norton became the white man, even though he was black. He became the slave trader, the man who kept us down; he represented pork chops, now that was wild in itself.

These were the years of the seventies, when white folks felt so bad for all the discrimination that had been heaped on blacks that Affirmative Action became the catch word of the day. Being black you could go to college for free, and a lot of the wrong people did. You had the street corner boys up there, it was almost like North Philly, then you had inner city youths from New York, it was wild. You also had the Greeks, the fraternity's and the sororities. They were like the privileged, everybody wanted to join them. Nevertheless you had to pay a terrible price, it was called pledging, it was a 12 week ordeal in which you were humiliated in public, they called it hazing, and your big brothers controlled you like a puppet. And not only that, but they were able to invite Greeks from other colleges to come up and humiliate you. You suffered from sleep deprivation, and all sorts of hazing and terror. I had a first hand experience with this process as my roommate during my junior year was a member of Kappa-Alpha-Phi fraternity. His order was for the pledges to bring him a hoagie from a particular store in Oxford Pa. He wanted this sandwich every night, so the pledges had to walk the four miles to Oxford every night. Now that was a dangerous trip in the day time because Oxford was a very prejudiced place, and the people that lived there for the most part. Many of them hated black people. They hated the fact that Lincoln University was there, so close to their town, so close to their living space. One night the Klux-Klux-Clan burned a cross on the campus of Lincoln University. That was Klan country that we lived in. But in retrospect, they had a right to dislike students from the college. We would go to town in bunches and try to rip the stores off, and steal anything we could get our hands on, we were not good ambassadors of the black race.

We actually reinforced what most white people thought about blacks. Once a friend of mines, Cliff went to Oxford with a group of us months earlier, our plan was to steal some radios from the local electronic store. He got caught; he was the only one who did get caught. He was supposed to pay a fine, but put it off until the end of the school year. He was waiting for his father to pick him up when the Pennsylvania State Troopers appeared at his door to arrest him. His dad showed up about twenty five minutes later looking to take Cliff home. I had to be the one to tell him that he had to pick Cliff up at the state troopers' barracks. There were other signs that there was racial discrimination. A fellow student was returning to Lincoln from the Christmas break, when someone pushed a boulder through the windshield of her father's car, her face was disfigured from the shattering glass, her medical bills were astronomical. So we got together and put on a series of concerts to raise money for her. The famous came to donate their time, all types of entertainers, we had groups like Rufus, with Chaka Chan, Kool and the Gang, everyone answered the call and we raised a lot of money for her. We had all types of students at Lincoln. African nations would send their best and brightest student to be educated there. This was the school where Thurgood Marshall went to, and the president of Ghana and many influential black people in the world. The African students really believed they were better than American blacks, like we were trying to be what they were, from the motherland or something. So here I was with all these diverse people, and I felt like I didn't belong. Those same feelings of low self-esteem, worthlessness that had plagued me all my life, so what did I do? I continued to get high that's what. This self destructive behavior continued until I returned to Philadelphia from Washington D.C. and got the job at the Institute for Behavioral Research.

5

Learning To Use Drugs.

I no longer wanted to be a research scientist as the experience at the institute had changed all that. The best thing that I got from my experience at The Institute of Behavioral was working with Pete as I stated in chapter three. Nevertheless, the experiments that we performed on the moneys were horrible. They each had their own personality, and were almost human. They sort of knew when their time was coming, and then there were the problems with the animal rights groups. The broke into the lab and let all the monkeys loose, they were all over Silver Spring Maryland, and we had to catch them. Then there were the secret government experiments that took place at Litton Bionetics in Rockville Maryland. You would be surprised to see what the government does with the taxpayer's money. The lab bought monkey fetus's, and we operated on the pregnant monkey, took out the fetus and while it was still attached to the umbilical cord. We would sever ganglia that was attached to the spinal cord and put the fetus back in the mother and continue the gestation period and allow the monkey to be born. This was to study birth defects and the regenerative ability of the spine and nervous system. Of course none of the monkeys lived beyond a few days. The monkey fetus's cost ten thousand dollars apiece, what a waste of money, but the government paid it.

So I came back to Philadelphia like I said disillusioned, and decided I needed a career change. Something new was coming, and there would be a lot of opportunity, it was called the personal computer, and it would change the world! I remember the Super Bowl commercial for nineteen eighty four, the one where the guy runs into the room with an Olympic torch, for Apple Computers. I enrolled at the Philadelphia Training Center and received a certificate in computer operations. My instructor, Earl, left to take a job running a computer store in West Philadelphia, at an Ivy League school. When I completed my course he hired me. My drug use escalated at this point. I was exposed to a new group of people. I went from just using and selling reefer, to being introduced to cocaine. There were two receptionists working at the computer store. They were heavy into cocaine, so as a token of their esteem, they introduced me to the drug. It started out as social usage. We would go to parties together and they introduced me to some influential people. It seemed as though the popular culture or our generation was involved with social use of cocaine. Just as the generation of the fifties were involved with heroin use. It was a natural progression, to go from one drug to another as well as a social progression. Nevertheless I should have known better, for I had all the warning that anyone needed, for my two younger brothers were already smoking cocaine, they called it freebasing. Many a time I watched them do it, and looked but did not see the reaction of their addictions to this substance. My brother William had a good job with Conrail, and the drugs took that away from him. I watched as his family fell apart, as his supplier would come all times of the day and night to supply drugs to him and my brother Donald. But in my mind, I told myself that I wasn't smoking cocaine only snorting which was more socially accepted.

So we went to parties and we tooted cocaine on our lunch breaks, I mean I was making good money then, and all we would get for our money was a little piece of aluminum foil containing this white powder, this girl as they called it. Man this was to me a miracle drug; I could go in the bathroom, take a toot and come out of the bathroom a new man. I could overcome all my social deficiencies with this white powder. I was more confident, more charismatic with this drug in my system. I felt as if I belonged. I wasn't the social geek that I always felt I was. I was masculine, I was the man. Soon everyone was stealing from the computer store. The receptionist, one was white one was black, I can't give their names, they were spending money like crazy. Nevertheless as the life got better it began it began to change. The world of drugs was always there, and I was indulging in more than just the weed.

As I began to snort cocaine, my whole world was about to come tumbling down. And that my friend is how the beginnings of a debilitating drug addiction starts. The drug at first gives you something, and I'm going to break it down so that even the people who never used drugs can understand. The drug gives the person who is using it something that is missing in their life. It diabolically figures out what that something is and sets about to rectify what is missing. We give it a lot of help, we addicts. If were not confident, and then the drug makes us confident. If we lack low self esteem, the drug, and this is the diabolical part, it gives you higher self-esteem, but only to the point that needs to get you addicted, then it removes any semblance of any kind of esteem, high, medium or low. Ever see that guy pushing that shopping cart, that girl selling her body? Did you ever wonder how they got that way? Well this is how because the drugs are willing to share you with your friends, your family, your children, your job and your humanity, then it takes that away from you when you can no longer do anything about it. That's when it's got you, bam, code-x, end of game and end of days.

The job itself was a good job, and we all just fucked it up. I was on the way up. I bought a house, had a new car, so I was living some semblance of the American dream, and by this time I had custody of my nephew, William Jr., as his fathers' drug addiction had enveloped him and the children's mother. This thing will split up families, it is merciless, and it wants all you got and then some. I had a new car, I had arrived. I was going to clubs, making up for lost time by fucking every beautiful girl I could get my hands on. Drinking Harvey's Bristol Crème sherry, and snorting up Peru. I had been a virgin until I was 21 years old; my virginity was taken by a neighbor that lived where I grew up at. She was older than me and very sexy, she had a reputation in the neighborhood; she was married but cheated on her husband very chance she got. She would stand on her porch and as we walked from the basketball court she would be dressed very sexy. Sometimes she would come down to the basketball court to get her sons for dinner wearing very revealing clothes. So one day I was walking home with my friends and I had my shirt off it was very hot, she must have saw my chest and she started to check me out. So she calls me over to her porch and I get her phone number. I shortly after that incident moved into my own apartment, so she stops by and we had sex, she said that she would teach me everything that I needed to know about sex and she did, she was very good at what she did. But this was the calm before the storm, for I was on the cusp of a personal Armageddon, and did not have a clue as to what was coming.

But there was good to in my life, I hooked up with a couple of neighborhood friends of mine, Charles Green and Acie Patterson, and we started a basketball league to help the neighborhood and relieve the tensions due to the gang violence. The summer basketball league was at the new playground 15th and Clearfield Streets. We had been given a playground by the city after years of neglect, the first playground was built around the corner from the new one and it was built on the same lot as a row home. Can you imagine that? It was so small, like playing basketball in someone's living room. We got many scars and left much skin on the wall of the playground. The out of bounds for the tiny basketball court was the walls on each side of the court, which were the remains of the walls from the row houses on each side of the court and the fence at each end was out of bound that way. Once Buddy Scott who lived down the street from me on Toronto Street could not stop on a drive to the basket and ran into the wall. He left his eyebrow from above his right eye on the walls lower half but he kept playing, we were warriors, you had to be a warrior to play there. So the new playground when it was finally built was a Godsend. The basketball league gave our neighborhood pride and attracted the best talent from Philly, guys like Rico Washington, Sugar Bear from Ben Franklin high school and gave the way where we grew up an identity. The teams were good too; we had the Super Hooper's, The Playboys, and outstanding local talent like the two Robinson brothers, Sed and Kevin, my brother Doug, Junkie and a host of other. There was still violence, once at a game these guys came down and shoot up the playground and a young person was injured. I remember holding the person and assuring him that he would be all right as the ambulance came, I no longer ran and was not afraid anymore. From the basketball league came Way Day, now everyone has a way that they remember from growing up. Somewhere you felt comfortable at, where everybody knows your name, and you're all just the same, and who dose not want to be where everybody knows your name. But thing were changing for me. I was still selling weed at the games, and using drugs.

I was living a deviant lifestyle outside the norm of society at large and did not really care. All that I cared about was about to disappear in a puff of smoke, like some cheap magicians trick , not all at once mind you but slowly, so slow that you cannot comprehend what is happening to you. Getting back to the store where I worked everyone was stealing computers, the original manager had left, Earl, and he was followed by a string of incompetent managers that made it so easy for everyone to stick their finger in the pie. The university had no idea what the inventory was, so we just did what drug addicts did. One thing is that the two receptionists were always traveling, they were going to exotic spots, and they were going to the Bahamas, England, Spain, and France on a daily basis. It never occurred to me how they were doing this on their receptionist salary, but they were. They would treat us to breakfast; I mean they were rolling in doe. One white girl was going with this black guy, and they were buying up property in University City and renovating it. They had an arcade in their basement. It was wild, and the sister was treating me and introducing me to powerful drug dealers. My cocaine use shot up. Unlimited money, young and single, it was the life!

Crack Cocaine:

Then the hammer dropped. The University did an audit at the store, and they found that they were missing hundreds of thousands of dollars worth of inventory. By this time a drastic change had taken place in my life. I was introduced to smoking cocaine by this girl I was dating at the time, her name was Denise and she was a beautiful black sister who caught up in smoking crack cocaine. So to be with her I tolerated her addiction, and enabled her by supplying her with the money for her addiction. I would by her drugs and paraphernalia and wait downstairs while she and her sisters smoked crack. But the real enlightenment came from my brother. As I said I had his son, so he would watch him while I worked. And every time I went to pick him up after work, there would be people partying, white, black, young and old. My brother William had what is known as a crack house, where you can go and smoke in a safe environment without the fear of being robbed, or hurt, so people came from all over all they had to do is pay house, which is a term that means you pay the persons whose house it is for the comfort of smoking there. Nevertheless, my brother William having an outgoing personality, everyone gravitated to him and his house to abuse drugs, myself included, and I mean everyone would go over there to smoke. Now being very observant , the always seemed to be having fun, married couples loving each other and the crack, one big happy family. But I never stayed around to see what happened after the money was gone, when the party was over, when the degradation took over, when they started to sell their watches, max out their credit cards, and sell their bodies. The party part looked harmless, so at my brothers urging I took a blast. Now I had tried it before, but never got anything out of it. They say that all you need is that perfect hit, the one you feel in your soul, the one that triggers that spot in your brain that affects the pleasure principal that releases the endorphins that triggers your addiction. The hit that is better than sex, which changes you forever. I got that hit that day and God help me it was the beginning of the end!

I became another person after that initial hit of crack, not all at once but slowly, because that is how addiction works. It is very patient, addiction does not want to scare you away by showing you what it is all about, so it works very slowly, but the change is evident. My habits changed at work it was more important to smoke crack than earn a living. So after the audit, the district attorney's office came down to investigate, and sure enough the evidence was there. The two receptionists had been funneling computers to this black guy who had his own computer store where he would resell them. They looked at a list of all the computers sold and matched it with the list of all the students, staff and faculty at the school. Any name not on the school list was a phony. Not only that but they used phony names like George Washington, Abe Lincoln and so forth. The girls had left a paper trail; they were arrested and given probation. The guy who owned the store that purchased the computers went to jail. I was much more careful and smarter than that so I was not caught.

So like I said, I was living the American Dream, or so I thought. I had bought a new home for me and my nephew to live in. I had bought a new Volvo; I had clothes, money, and women and really intended to do the right thing. I was dating the head cashier at the bookstore, Tina. She was a wonderful person but at the time I met her addiction was growing stronger and stronger. I had graduated from the simple tooting cocaine up my nose to smoking it, which was a completely different experience and animal. You see, there were people who were freebasing as they called it for years, which is buying raw cocaine in the powder form and cooking it. I tried that, buying the powder and cooking it, but I could never get it right in the beginning, I wasted a lot of money going to cop and coking it myself. What I needed was cocaine that was already cooked, and someone provided that. It was called "Crack cocaine". This really took drug addiction to a new level, it put shit in the game so to speak, and it also opened Pandora's Box. This new shit, this crack made it easy and inexpensive for drug addicts to get and use. Crack cocaine helped to mass produce drug addicts; it took the casual user and turned them into a raving maniac. Crack affected the brain in such a way that there was no more casual user, the functional addict was turned into the longer able to function as a human being addict It was to become the scourge of the twentieth century. I really believe that in the future, the history of mankind will include this saga of our existence. This drug addiction that is happening in our lifetime will be talked about, and it will ultimately reveal how we almost destroyed ourselves. This drug addiction problem that we are living through will be looked back upon as a dark time for all of us and those who had survived it will be recognized for going through hell and making it back alive.

Crack cocaine had to come from a laboratory, because there is no way that something this powerful and harmful could be naturally produced by nature, only man in all of his destructiveness could have invented something so sinister. It was nothing like the cocaine that preceded it. It affects the mind and pushes the buttons that will make you do anything for it. You will forsake your children and family. You will sell your body parts, your blood and your soul if they paid cash for it somewhere. It is heinous and devious; it is an equal opportunity addiction. It pays no mind to race, color or creed. It is unprejudiced, it is not sexist or a racist, it takes all who dare to answer its call, and it will kill as many as possible. What it does is that it robs you of your humanity, little by little, and when we lose our humanity we become empty shells, husk of flesh and bone, suffering and set apart from the rest of mankind, separated from our spirituality, so alone, so alone. This addiction separates each addict, even from other addicts. There is only room in your life for crack first and you second. All the things you say that you will never do, you do. There is no limit, no bottom. It effects on such a base level that even when you get clean, it still haunts you like a shell shocked war survivor. I still am not right with myself. God help me.

It's so painful to deal with the memories, the reality of what crack did and what it did to my family, I can only write about that in small doses, then I must get away from the memories, least I be consumed again. My inner demons still exist and I will carry them for the rest of my life, they are even now waiting and lurking, looking for a way to re-ignite the fires of my addiction so that it can destroy me once again. Nevertheless, I was dating this wonderful woman whose names were Tina, and keeping my addiction from her, my co-workers and family. You know how you sometimes look back on your life and there was the perfect person for you, the one you should have been with the rest of your life? Well Tina was that someone for me. In each of our lives, God will give us the perfect mate, but most of us never achieve the happiness that could come from that perfect relationship. We mess it up, the person dies, or we just do not act properly to insure that person stays in our lives but we each get a chance I believe, and it's up to us what we do with it. We would go out to hotels to spend the night and I would hide in the bathroom and smoke crack while she thought I was taking a shower. We went out to dinner, to concerts but the psychological effects of the drugs were beginning to tell on me. The isolation was becoming more and more of who I was. And my addiction was not willing to share me with her or anyone. She had a beautiful home up in Yeadon Pennsylvania; she was a widow with a beautiful grown daughter she was searching for herself after her husband died. Tina worked in the bookstore at the University of Pennsylvania and I worked in the computer store, I met for the first time as I was cashing my paycheck, she worked in the bursar's office. She cashed checks, sold tokens and just looked beautiful doing it; she was truly a creature of God. I know now that she really loved my, I should of married her and moved into the house with her, but cocaine had other plans for me and for us. So I began to draw away from her, as the addiction became stronger it caused my feelings for Tina to grow weaker. Tina, being very naïve to what was happening had no idea as to why my behavior was changing and after I left the bookstore we stopped communicating altogether, God I miss her, even to this day, but I wish her well. I went to see her years later after I had gotten clean, I by now had my custody of my daughter, so I took her with me, she did not seem to interested, perhaps she was still angry about what had happened between us years a go, I do not know but the fire was definitely out. Oh she was still civil to me but that was that, though I still thought that I had to try just to put that part of my life to rest.

Nevertheless, the drugs began to take over my life, I can remember sitting in my house with the doors locked smoking crack to the point of being paranoid and out of my mind. I was so paranoid that I would begin to hear people downstairs in my house when there were no people. I remember sitting with my shotgun loaded next to me smoking my brains out, and keep having to go downstairs to check on who was sneaking up on me. I would move the refrigerator so that it blocked the cellar door because that is where I was sure they were coming from. "They", who the hell were they? They were the demons within me coming to consume me, the ever growing paranoid psychosis that was fueled by the crack cocaine. It was the guilt I felt every time I got high as my morals, values and sense of right and wrong battled with the demon of addiction and lost every time. It was the guilt for failing me and my nephew and my family. Guilt is a very powerful emotion as we all know, it can cause us to act outside of ourselves, but guilt can also be medicated, put to sleep that is the only way to continue something as self destructive as an addiction. I would take a hit in the basement and hear people coming for me I would hear people on the porch, my neighbors, the mailman; they were all coming for me. The paranoia would be so great that it threatened to consume me, and on a few occasions it almost did. Listening for voices, hearing voices coming from somewhere, not really sure where, but the voices where there. Maybe they were in my head, or maybe they were not, but they were there, I was sure of it. At this point I believe that my sanity was being compromised by my addiction, but the monkey on my back told me to keep going, to grind it out, fuck everything.

Any drug addict who tells you that he or she is enjoying their respective addiction is lying to you through their teeth. You do not enjoy your addiction; you just live with it you exist with it. It takes you give and that's how it plays out. I remember when the addiction became so bad, and the slipping into darkness began. I had my nephew living with me, and I began to not be able to offer him a good quality of life. I began to expose him to the very things I had so nobly sought to rescue him from. I had him in school, but I had stopped working because the job was getting in the way. I wanted to be a full time addict and the job was in the way. I remember it as if it were yesterday, the people at my job knew that something was wrong with me. My performance had slipped. I was careless and not paying attention to detail. The job suspected a drug problem, and offered to get me help. There was a meeting in the manager's office of the Penn bookstore and they approached me about getting help. Well my addiction told me to tell them where to go, which was straight to hell and I quit my job. I remember the words coming out of my mouth, but not really saying them, but deep down inside I got what I wanted. So now I could become a full time addict. I had money in the bank a new home and car, I would be alright, or so I thought. I got a job with a friend that I had worked with at the computer store; he opened his own business in Ardmore Pa. I was high as a kite every day. I would race back to my house on my lunch break to smoke crack, then race back to work; only I was getting back from lunch later and later. I had to drive over twelve miles each way from Ardmore Pennsylvania on City Line Avenue to route 76 and get off at Broad Street and from there go to my house and once I got there I had to hope the dealers were open so that I could get the crack and smoke it and drive the twelve miles back to work. I had control over testing and building computers for the customers so I had an office that was separate from the main store. Even with this much lead way, the job was getting in the way, just like before, so I quit that job too. I was thirty-two years old, and about to embark on a journey that would last for the next eight years, a journey that would lead to a downward spiral from which there would be no coming back, for many years. It was the beginning of my end, I just could not see it, and I was blinded by my addiction to crack. The money in the bank went; I sold my car and smoked that up.

I then took in a tenant, it was a guy I worked with named Ken, he was a very racist guy and hated Jewish people, but he paid and I tolerated   his racist remarks because I needed more money to get high. Ken was a Vietnam War vet and kind of crazy, he was also white. Ken was German American and he hated Jewish people, he would make all kinds of sadistic jokes about Jews and I would laugh, just to be his friend, I think that he liked black people, or to put it this way, he tolerated black people, he did not hate them as much as Jewish people. I am sure that the experience of Vietnam had damaged him psychologically in some way; he was a very bitter dude. But he knew computers and was very good with the Macintosh computer that we sold from Apple computers; you see Ken also worked at the Computer store on Penn's campus. So he moved in with me and he kept a lot of money in his room, I broke into his room and stole the money to get high, I told him the house got robbed, I even broke the hall window to make it look like a break in, I was really sick, but I would continue to do this until he moved out, then I was left with no means of income.

Why is it that the drug addicts is always the last to know that he or she is not fooling anyone, that people who don't use drugs can always tell when you are high? When I took my car to the Volvo dealership on north Broad Street, I thought that I could fool them into thinking that I was not an addict. Well they took advantage of the situation and gave me three thousand dollars and an old car for my new car. I gladly took it and smoked it up, then I went back and they gave me money for brakes on the trade in and I smoked that up. Then I started to rent my car out to drug dealers, and they fucked it up, the drug dealers would give me crack to use my car and this one young drug dealer would shift the car while driving it, except the car was an automatic transmission, and he messed up the transmission, so the car would only run in reverse and that was the end of my car. My utilities got turned off, and I remember bathing my nephew with water heated up in the electric fry pan. I started to do odd jobs, and was working for a friend of mines uncle who sold drugs. We were cleaning out a building that he had bought, and then he would give us drugs as payment. I was cleaning the roof when I fell through the sky light that was covered with leaves, I could not see it. I tore my hand up on the jagged glass, and fell two stories to the floor below. It was like a Three Stooges episode or something, you know where they fall from a tremendous height and hit the ground and they get up and are alright? Well that is what is like for me when I fell through the skylight. We had to stop working, and then we went to get paid. So after getting paid, some in money and some in crack, instead of going to the hospital to get my hand stitched up, my friend and I went back to my house to smoke the crack. The blood gushed through my hand with each pull on the pipe, I almost bleed to death but didn't care, and I went to the hospital when the crack was gone and not before and I almost lost my hand, I had wrapped my hand up with a sheet that was drenched in blood by the time we got to the hospital.

There was another time when I tried to sell my house to a drug dealer even though the mortgage was already in default, so I really had nothing to sell him, but he didn't know that. So I strung him along, getting cocaine from him until he found out. He was on his way to kill me when he got sent back to jail for a parole violation it was another lucky break for me. God really looked after me during my addiction. I came so close to death so many times, but he always protected me. I also continued to sell all of my worldly possessions, everything that was dear to me, I would take my jazz record collection down to a drug dealer named Fonze and he would give me crack for them, I sold everyone of them. I even walked them down to a record store on South Street, the guy was not there to but those, so I left them there, I later saw where he had put them up for sale. I was too high to do anything about it, also to cowardly. I would also sell my computer books to any bookstore that would buy them, once I forced my nephew Jay to walk with me to Red Lion Road to this bookstore, it was so hot we almost did not make it there and once we got there the guy that bought the books was off for the day. I was devastated, so there we were with no way to get back, and I had to give my precious books to a cab driver to take us home.

During this time, my grandfather died, his name was Mr. Lonnie Ballard. He was quite a character, and I loved him very much. He never had a bad thing to say about anyone, and was always there for me and my family. I cannot really remember much more than that except to say he died of colon cancer. He was healthy one day, and when he was diagnosed with the cancer, of course he had surgery and after the surgery he got worse. He was bedridden as the cancer ate him away. My grandmother put a hospital bed down in the living room for him, as he could not get up and down the stairs anymore. It is all so hazy because the drugs really had a hold of me by then, and it still seems like a blur but all I can remember was that he died, and that I was too high to go to the funeral, can you imagine that? Too high to go to your grandfather's funeral and being okay with it from a human perspective, this is something else that I must deal with and must ask my grandfather's and God's forgiveness. Life got worse for us both my nephew and I, the mortgage was not getting paid, so the eviction notices started to come which I of course ignored. Nevertheless after about a year of ignoring the eviction notices they came to evict me. One day when I was getting high with my best friend Clayton there was a knock at the door and it was the sheriff and a moving van; they gave me fifteen minutes to get as many of my belongings as I could carry, they were putting me out forcibly. I will tell you, when that truck pulls up, it is no more procrastinating, you are out, either you leave on your on accord, or they put you out. I was messing up not only my life, but the life of my young nephew, William or Jay as he was called He was along on this addiction ride right with me.

I was being forcibly evicted, but by then I had sold everything in the house that could be sold. I tore up the basement so that I and a friend of mine could get the washer and dryer out to sell to a second hand store, we tore the air conditioner out of the wall and boarded up the hole and sold the air conditioner to a drug dealer. I sold every thing I had. I was a frequent visitor to this badlands; which was located at 8th and Butler streets. I sold my movies, clothes, pots pans even my potholders went. It was a going out of my mind sale .By this time the quality of life that I could give my nephew William Jr., was sinking deeper and deeper. He was suffering and I did not care to acknowledge that. He was not being cared for properly as my addiction got worse and I was powerless to do any thing about it and my apathy set in. We were eating from an electric griddle, as the gas was turned off. He would go to school and I would spend the whole day getting high, cook him some Oodles of Noodles and resume getting high while he played outside. I would take him with me as I copped on the way home from work after I picked him up from my grandmothers house. God, he was so young, and saw so much of the wrong things, everything bad that he went through; I must accept the fact that it is my fault. Once I bought him a bicycle, and when the money ran out, my friend Zandy and I stole the bike off the porch and took it to his uncle who sold drugs, and sold the bike to him for drugs, and later told Jay that his bike was stolen from the porch, now how sick is that? I have done so much wrong, to so many people that I can only ask God to forgive me. Sometimes it swells up inside me and I want to cry, but I have to live with these memories, and the effect it had on everyone that my life touched. I was a piece of shit, and did not care that I hurt, nor was I concerned about the path my life was following, all I cared about was getting high.

6

The Beginning of the End.

The end never comes quickly, and it never comes all at once, the end always comes slowly, sneaks up on you, and for me losing my home was the end result of years of not being responsible. It was the end result of rampant crack cocaine use, of lies, and deceit, of abuse to me and my nephew. It was the result of the spiritual decay, the moral decay and the intellectual decay that my drug abuse had wrought. It was the harvest that I had to reap for the way I had chosen to live my life. Nevertheless when it came it came very quickly and I had to pretend that I did not see it coming, so when the sheriffs knocked on the door with the police and told me to leave, I had to pretend that I was shocked, I had to pretend to myself that they had the wrong house, the wrong guy. It was my name on the eviction notice, but it had to be a mistake I thought, and besides they had ruined my high, I had just taken a hit of crack before the sheriff arrived. Nevertheless it was not a mistake and to my surprise it was me that they were looking for, they had the right person, it was only in my drug addicted mind that they had the wrong person.

I was taken with all my processions to my grandmother's house, to my Nana; now let me tell you about my Nana .I had talked about Nana earlier in the book when I was talking about my childhood, she was a complex woman; she was my father's mother. She was always there when the family needed here, and would do anything for her grand-children, but she was the kind of person who would remind you what she did, and my father hated that. Who wouldn't? Whenever there was a bill to be paid, food to be put on the table, a holiday like Christmas or

Easter, she came along, and with my mother's mother Mom-mom they would come to the rescue. Not that my parents, really my dad weren't good providers, it was just to many of us for any two parents to handle, so my Mom-mom and my Nana would have to come to the rescue. So I went back to her house I took my addiction with me, and my nephew Jay and she let us back in. Nana had custody of young James, Jay's younger brother, he was also the son of my brother William Sr. He was a troubled young child, from birth, sort of sickly, they did not expect him to live, but he did. He was always in trouble, not a bad child, but a perfect example of what is happening in our city today, as well as the black society as a whole. He was not given the guidance he needed at an early age, and was also bereft of love and nurturing as his parents addiction had really taken off by the time he was born. My grandmother took him from my brother and his mother because he was being neglected and not being fed as a baby, lying in his crib neglected, with a dirty diaper on him. You see this is the tragedy and the toll that drug addiction takes on the black race. So he grew up mischievous , and by the time I got there I was in no shape to help mold his young mind or set a positive example, I owe James too, God please add him to the list of people that I have failed. By this time Nana was beginning to show the signs of Alzheimer's disease. She was beginning to lose her memory, she also suffered from diabetes, high blood pressure and had an inoperable tumor in her stomach, Nana's body was breaking down and the doctors could do nothing to help her because she was dying. A long list of people passed through her house at this time, most of them were addicts. She never turned away someone in need; they were taking advantage along with me of her good nature. These people that were staying at Nana's house were stealing her money, not paying her rent, and just taking advantage of her old age and her being ill, and I did nothing to stop it, I was so caught up in my addiction that I really didn't care. And I did my dirt to which of course I am very ashamed of, but I have to live with this.

Once I was arrested because I went to the store for Nana to buy a pound of lunchmeat, I stopped before going to the store to buy a vial of crack. On the way back to the store I was stopped by a police wagon with two female officers in it. They jumped out and one shouted "Run and I will shoot you"; they searched me and found the trey or three dollar vial of crack so I was arrested and taken to the Roundhouse. I had another three dollar vial of crack in my socks, and for the next twelve hours, my task was to hide this crack in my sock so that I could smoke it when the police released me from jail. I walked with this vial rubbing against me foot for twelve hours, waiting to see the judge and be arraigned so that I could go home and smoke this crack. Finally I was released and ran to fifteenth and Poplar streets from eighth and Race Streets, and climbed in the second floor bathroom window, went into my room and smoked the crack; I never did get the lunch meat.

Her brother, my great uncle hired this addict to take care of her, his name was Randy. He was one of the worst dope fiends that I have ever seen He was smart, cunning and knew how to get in with old folks, being from Mississippi, he was folksy, a homey kind of nigger, and the old folks loved him, while he robbed them blind. There was a lady that lived across the street from Nana, her name was Miss. Lovie. Nana and she had been friends for years, so Randy got in good with her, he would run errands, fix things around Miss Lovie's house, one day Randy found this money that Miss Lovie was saving; she had it stashed in paper bag hidden in the chimney. A lot of older people that age did not believe in banks so they kept their money in their houses. Well Randy found her life savings and stole every penny of it and smoked it up on crack, Miss Lovie died before she found out it was missing, but that was the type of addict that Randy was. I met him on the farm and we were both going to pick Blueberries. He was a good crook and had a scam where he was getting multiple food stamps allotments using social security numbers from his home town in Mississippi, he showed me how to do it and we began to rip off the system. He was also a very bad person, no more than most of us as we fall prey to our illness, I guess. He began to steal everything in my grandmother's house, and selling it. A lifetime of mementos, everything that made my grand-mothers house what it was, he stole and sold. He was given free rein because no one else wanted to be bothered, it took so much to take care of her and we could not afford a nursing home for her, and let me say that it was such a difficult task to care for Nana, Uncle Herman and Aunt Carrie did the best they could for her. It was other people that did not step up to the plate like my father and I included.

It was just an overwhelming situation for other elderly people to see someone they love deteriorate like that. She began not to be able to recognize people, she became bedridden, and had to be waited on hand and foot. I will admit this even though he stole from her, he did the best he could in taking care of her. Randy to his defense he bathed her and fed her. Randy was found shot in the head a short time after that, he pulled one scam too many on some drug dealers and they killed him for it. The police found him bound and gagged in an old garage at 15th and Parrish Streets. By this time I was at this time spending a lot of time at my brothers William's house. I had a job at the local bar down the street from his house cleaning up on Saturday's, and then I would smoke the money up. The manager of the bar, she sold large amounts of cocaine, I used to steal from the bar whatever I could sell even pennies for this huge jar. I was at my brothers' house that Saturday morning, when one of my youngest brother's Alex called to say that Nana had died that morning, I was high as a kite when I heard, and I came down very quickly. I rushed home and they were just taking her body out of the house, my nephews were there and had to deal with this without me, I had let them down again I got high some more, It was the beginning of the worst period of my life.

My Demise:

After they buried my Nana, I was left with her house; I had the boy's James and Jay, my two nephews' and I proceeded to teach them all that I knew that was wrong about life. As my drug addiction grew, I was receiving welfare for them; they had to go to the welfare line with me to receive my benefits so I wouldn't smoke it all up. They had to miss school so they were assured that they would get a pair of sneakers, or that I would buy food. By that time they had turned the water off because the line from the street had ruptured and we could not afford to get it fixed, so we lived out of the fire hydrant. All our drinking water came from the fire hydrant, water to flush the toilet, to drink, to cook with; they also turned off the gas, so we cooked on a hotplate. No matter if it was holidays or birthdays, everyday was the same. The world had lost its meaning, and life had lost its meaning, there was no today or no tomorrow, I was living in a whirlwind of mistrust and deceit. I was in freefall, and my life was in ruins. I was living in hell and could not get out, so I embraced this life of evil and became a part of it. I was a willing part of this whole scene, and I loved it. I was trapped in this nightmare and could not get out. I disgraced the memory of my grandmother and her home, my mother and father, my sisters my brothers, my in-laws and outlaws. And the worst was yet to come!

7

Crime School.

When I was a child, I watched a movie called "Crime School", starring Humphrey Bogart and James Cagney. It was about a group of juveniles called The Dead End Kids who were growing up in New York, a section called "Hell's Kitchen", and the effect that this environment had on these children. I thought years later, what a name for a place, 'Hell's Kitchen", it must have been quite a place, well "Hell's Kitchen had nothing on this misery I am about to unfold for you. Right there at 15th and Ogden Streets we had our own version of crime school, run by me. What I proceeded to do; and I am ashamed to say I did it, but I not only ruined my life, but also the lives of three of my nephews. They were Omar, James and Jay. Everything bad about their lives; I have to take responsibility for, because as my addiction grew worse, after my grandmother died, I became a dysfunctional role model. I tried to take care of them but I couldn't take care of myself. So I was always up at the school, because James was out of control, I was always walking around at night looking for them in the summer time because it was way too late for them to be out, and I ran out of get-high.

Down On the Farm:

James became so delinquent that my older sister Sharon had to have him placed in a home for problem children. Nevertheless the damage was done, his chance for a normal life was ruined, and it would play itself out to its predictable end some years later. So that left me with my nephews Omar and Jay, I began to fall in with drug dealers. Oh I tried other means to support my habit like when I was a child, my mother would pack up all her children and take us all to New Jersey to work on the farms picking blueberries and tomatoes because we needed the money. Dad would be gone on one of his excursions, and we would go to make money. It was very hot; and you only got paid for what you picked. The buses were filled with the elderly trying to make ends meet, the winos trying to support their habits, and families like ours trying to survive. So I went back to the farms in my addiction in the summertime and you know what? Not much had changed since I was a child, it was still hot, and you only got paid for what you picked, but I was more motivated, I was working for crack money, and the winos were still there but we crack addicts outnumbered them. Then you had the girls who went to the farm so that they could sell their bodies in the fields. These girls would go on the buses too and take up a seat with no intention of picking anything; they would wait for you to pick your blueberries and try to sell you some ass in the bushes for your tickets. You had the people who ran the buses, they would charge outlandish prices for a chicken sandwich, or for a soda, they also sold beer and wine, their job was to take as much of your money as they could. They were not getting any of my money; I needed all that to get high with so I would take my lunch with me.

So on the way back the bus load of people would stop at the Happy House, which was a liquor store, they called it the Happy House because all of the winos would get real happy when we stopped and they got their booze. I would get me a bottle of Sisco wine and when we got back to the city I would stop in the projects and get my dope. I would stop and buy a pizza for the boys, and retire to my room to get high all night and get up without any rest and do it again the next day. Thus began the decade of the 90's, it all went by so fast. I would toil in the hot sun for twelve hours a day, for twenty nine dollars and smoke up that hard earned money, get up at five the next morning and do it again. Once on the bus I ran into a girl named Marcy who was an alcoholic, she told me she was working on the farm to get her brother out of jail, I thought that was admirable, here I was working to get high, and she was working to get her brother out of jail. It turns out that her brother was King Solomon on the King Solomon wine bottle, and the jail he was in was the state store. Marcy was also a thief, so once while every one was asleep; she crept to the back of the bus to steal a wine bottle that she thought had some wine in it. She grabbed the bottle and turned it up to her mouth and drunk it down without stopping to taste it. It turns out that the bottle she drank contained urine, that dark yellow urine, like monkey piss. The other winos had set her up, every one roared with laughter, every one except Marcy of course. Nevertheless the farm was a tough way to make a living because the job of the people who drove the buses that took you over to the farm, they worked with the farmer and both of their aims was to rip you off as much as possible. But we all chose to be there, so who could blame them; to them we were just addicts.

About this time I fell victim to a loan shark, he would hold my welfare card until check day, and then loan me dollar on the dollar, so for twenty dollars, I had to pay back forty dollars. His name appropriately enough was Worm and he had quite a operation, he head drivers who picked up the suckers like me, and escorted us to the welfare distribution center He always gave more back because he liked the boys that were living with me. He liked James and Jay, but he did not like it when his clients ran out on him and got a new welfare card and did not pay him. He once bought such a client to my house, it was some drug addict that they had caught after he ran out, and they paid me twenty dollars to break his leg in my house. Of course I jumped at the chance to earn twenty dollar and besides it was not my leg is the way I looked at it so I waited outside while they took him into the house, and after hearing Worm's verbal tirade, I heard the sickening sound of a baseball bat hitting flesh, and the screams that followed. Afterward Worm was very cordial as he asked the guy if he needed medial help, and they took him to Saint Joseph's hospital and dumped him out of the car. They would buy your food stamps seven dollars for ten dollars, they made it easier to get high, you could go through your welfare allotment in two days, and sometimes in two hours. The food stamps were supposed to last for a month, everything was up in smoke and this was the beginning of my end. Both as a human being and a role model, I was all morally bankrupt and devoid of spirit. My house became a magnet, a beacon for prostitution, drugs and gambling, it was a hit house. You know, you pay me to hit your drugs in my house.

Everything that I was was lost during this time. Everything I was taught, from the time that I was a child was lost during this time. All the time my family took to teach me the things that would make me a decent human being was wiped from my mind, like a computer that crashes with a virus .To be sure, theses things were leaving me over the years, a little at a time, but now, this was the coup de -gras, I had arrived and I was there. When people don't use drugs they often wonder, how can drug addicts be like that? How can the woman and men sell their bodies? How can they remain homeless? How can this and how can that be happening? I will try to explain, but unless you've been there, you will never truly understand. Not that I would wish this journey on anyone. For many do not survive. The addiction takes over. I believe that we are all hard wired to become addicts, coming from the same gene pool as we do, we are all the same. Take away the superficial out side appearances, like skin color, race, eye color, hair texture we are hard wired by our genes even from conception. We are all the same from one gene pool since humanity started from two individuals in Africa millions of years ago, and this hard wired behavior manifest itself in different ways in all of us. Some of us become workaholics, some of us become addicted to food some to alcohol and some of us become addicted to drugs.

By this time I was renting rooms to whores, like Mattie, and Angie for five dollars a half hour, they would bring in their tricks and I would make money off of the drug runs. Once Angie, a whore who lived on the second floor, had her boyfriend Khalif move in with her, they got into a fight and he bit her on the cheek, he bit her very deep because he did not want other guys to find her attractive, it seemed that there was always some drama going on, but it went with the territory. I would cook fried chicken legs on a hot plate and we would make sandwiches out of the chicken and the large Thomas's English muffins we would get from the shelter on Ridge Avenue. I ran into a boyhood friend, John from down the way, that I grew up with, he was in charge of giving out food at the shelter and would give us extra food. Nevertheless, he was battling his own demons, and would come around on the weekends after he got paid to trick and get high; it seemed that everyone was getting high. It never ceases too amaze me how much violence that we are capable of enduring, or how we can become adapted to the violence and how the violence can became an everyday thing. It became so much a part of our lives that we began to think that it was normal to live like we were living. I was never a violent person growing up, but I guess that human nature allowed me to become a part of the violence, to accept it. You rationalize that the daily beatings that you and other people endure are not the product of sane behavior, just so that you can continue the insanity of the drug use. I think that we were all sick to some degree, I am talking about the addict and the drug seller, we had a symbiotic relationship, and we both needed each other. We fed off of each others misery, the drug addict to prolong his disease and the drug dealer to prolong his illness, the illness that does not allow a person to want to lead a normal life. The sickness was pervasive and insidious, and neither of us realized how sick we were, that is the nature of the illness, you can convince yourself that you are doing alright. The drug dealer that sells you the drugs convinces himself that he is not responsible for the misery of the addict, and the addict believes that he is also not responsible for his or hers own misery.

So I continued to educate my nephews and to ruin their lives and mines in the process. It started when we were approached to sell drugs for one of the dealers in the neighborhood. It seemed like a way to make some quick money, and to fuel my addiction, so I agreed. We were already renting the rooms out to prostitutes for there tricks, five dollars for half an hour, and there was the Carlyle Hotel on Poplar street. They also rented rooms but for much more and when they were full and overflowed, it was money time for me. Now all this took place right across the street from my grandmother's former church, Second Pilgrim Baptist Church which was located at 15th and Ogden Streets, we just toned down the violence and drug selling on Sundays. I also went into my mountain man mode, I wouldn't bathe, or shave, and all I wanted to do was get high, I grew this long beard, looked like a cracked out Santa Claus. I began to work for the Philadelphia Daily News as one of there street hustlers, you know the guys you see out on the corner selling the Philadelphia Daily News or Philadelphia Inquirer, with the red newspaper boxes on wheels? Well I was one of them. I began working in West Philly. I had to get up at 5 a.m. to get to 30ᵗʰ street station to meet the crew boss, his name was Murphy, his only claim to fame was that he was married to the daughter of Kenny Gamble, of Gamble and Huff records, I guess has thought he was owed something for that, so anyway the inquirer truck would drop the papers off, and of we would go, traveling by subway or trolley to our destinations. I started on 34ᵗʰ and Market streets, a marginally busy intersection. I remember my sister Sharon and her husband Nelson would come Driving by, they would stop to buy a paper from me, I should have felt ashamed to be out there, but I wasn't, the crack took all the shame and pride I had, it had reduced me to pieces of a man as Gil Scott Herron had sang in the song Pieces of a Man.

Councilwoman Janine Blackwell was another customer; she would give me the whole dollar and tell me to keep the change, she was a tipper and there were not many of them. So I worked my way up to the big time, 58ᵗʰ and Baltimore Ave. Now that was a jumping corner, I could make sixty five dollars on a good day, and most of the days were good. I was out there in the rain or the snow, in the sunshine no matter how hot it was it did not matter to me. It was so bad in the winter time that I had to keep leaving the corner because my feet kept getting wet; I had on canvas sneakers and the melting snow kept leaking into my sneakers. So I had to keep going to the laundromat on the corner to dry my socks and sneaks in the dryer, I repeated this cycle for at least 10 times per day. I had to watch my cart because I had to leave it in the middle of the street and I was also afraid that I would miss my customers Then Murphy would come pick us up, we would hand in our money for the papers we sold, return the unsold papers, and the race was on to get back to North Philly, and to the drug man. I would get high all day, go to sleep, arise again at five a.m. to repeat the process. It lasted until I stole some money and was dismissed; I tried to pay him for less than the amount of papers that I sold.

About this time a very profound experience happened to me. I suffered from ulcers all through the seventies and the eighties. This is when doctors were guessing what caused ulcers, they did not know as they do now that ulcers were caused by a bacteria, every time I had a bad attack the doctors swore that I was drinking alcohol, but I was not drinking. I was given to bouts of illness where I couldn't eat for days at a time and sometimes it stretched into weeks. This one particular time, some of my friends from the suburbs came over to get high with me, they were cool white boys, and they bought a case of Moosehead beer with them. Now I am sick and I have not eaten for days, but I still wanted to get high, so I began making runs for them to buy crack and when I got back I was drinking beer. About 4 a.m. that morning, I became really ill, I doubled over and I could feel and hear what felt like air coming out of my stomach, like you hear when a tire springs a leak. And when the hissing sound stopped, I doubled over in pain and I began to vomit mouthfuls of blood, at this point one of my friends asks me, "can you go get some more crack" No I shouted, so they took their last hit and left as if I was going to die and they did not want to be around to witness my death. The pain intensified and I could hardly breathe, I knew that I was in trouble at this point. My nephew Omar had to call the police to take me to the hospital and when the police arrived, I was so doubled over in pain I could not stand up. So the police had to call the fire rescue wagon and they helped me into the van and took me first to Saint Joseph's hospital. When they determined that I needed surgery, they had to transfer me to Guiffre Hospital which was at eight and Girard Avenue. It being early Sunday morning I had to wait in the emergency room until the surgeon was found and bought back to the hospital. I lay in that hallway on a stretcher for what seemed like hours, in agony, they could not give me anything for the pain because I had drugs in my system. People walked by me, nurses, other doctors, and because I was a drug addict, no one seemed to care that I was in such pain; it was if I was invisible, or like I was the invisible man!

Finally, I was given a pain killer and taken to emergency surgery because the doctor had arrived. My ulcer had ruptured, and I had a hole in my stomach. The doctor had to remove part of my stomach and small intestine, I died I am told on the operating table twice, but they bought me back, I guess that it was not my time to go yet. I woke up in the Intensive care unit hours later. The hospital knew I was an addict by the cocaine that was in my system when they took my blood for testing. I was still trying to kill myself, but God kept intervening, he had a plan for me. I remained in the hospital for ten days, most of it with a pump running through my nose into my stomach to pump out the acid so that my stomach could heal from the staples that now held my stomach together. I thought that I would walk out of the hospital in a day or two, my addiction was still calling me, I tried to stand and couldn't, my body have undergone a traumatic experience, and all I still thought about was getting high. My sister Sharon who had the same surgery years earlier came to visit me and told me that I was not going anywhere soon, I didn't believe her, but I could not stand up. It took days before I could even sit in the chair next to my bed while the nurse changed my bed linens. I was on a liquid diet when I finally could eat and was so hungry that I ate a chocolate chip cookie from my roommate's dinner tray. I still had the tube going down my throat to drain the acid from my stomach and that was the reason that I was on a liquid diet. The cookie jammed up the pump and I had to be taken back into surgery, my doctor was very upset and said that I almost died again, but at this point I really did not care.

So they released me from the hospital in about a week, and my mother came to the hospital to get me and take me home. While I was in the hospital, the electricity at the house got turned off, as well as my welfare check. When I was released from the hospital, I could barely stand. My mother left me a battery operated radio, so I could listen to the news, and some candles for light, Omar and I spent the night in the dark. Nevertheless the first thing I did was scam this older lady who live across the street from me out of ten dollars, I told her I needed for a prescription, and walked up to the drug boys to cop, I needed a hit. But I could not find my pipe, it seems Omar had let someone use my pipe while I was in the hospital and they stole it so I had to use a makeshift metal pipe to smoke from I ended up wasting all of my crack. The next day I had to get the lights turned back on. So I had to go up to the

Department of Public Assistance office, and sit there for hours to get the money for the electricity to be turned back on. I had left the James and Jay with their father while I was in the hospital, and he wanted to be paid for watching them, can you imagine that! Nevertheless that is how it was, I was saved again by God and there was a reason why I was saved but I did not know about or care about, I just went back to doing my thing, which was ruing my life.

So I had to find an alternative way to make money to support my drug habit and I went to drug pushing. I began working for a local dealer named OT, He would have me run errands for him, I would drive his car and go get his weed, clean up dog shit after his dogs, and do whatever he wanted me to do, In payment he would give me a few vials of crack, because he was on house arrest OT could not go out, he was waiting to be sentenced to jail on a drug charge. OT came from a family of drug dealers; he learned drug dealing from his father who was also a drug dealer. If we are not careful we pass all that bad shit that we do on to our children n because in most cases our children become what we are, OT's brothers and sisters also sold drugs, they were one big happy drug selling family. So I spent the next year doing running errands for OT, but I did meet my daughters mother while dealing with OT, she was one of his girls, and had a major drug habit. Get this she had left her three children with their father, disowned them to get high, that's how powerful crack is. Nevertheless, OT had full custody of his young daughter and he really took care of her and loved her, I remember many a time I would arrive at his house and see him doing his daughter's hair himself.

So after OT was sentenced and went to jail his daughter went to live with his sister, and I had to find another way of supporting my habit so we began to sell drugs for Lamont. Lamont was an enterprising young man, he was still in high school; he would drop off drugs on his way to school, and pick the money up after school. I met him through my nephew Omar, and he also knew Jay, so we set up shop, it was a million dollar operation. Although I say very little of it I got paid with crack. Even Lamont's mother and father were addicts, one time she came around in the middle of the night and demanded the drugs on her son's orders, she was tripping, so we gave her some and Lamont dealt with her the next day. But she was crazy to think that she could get away with that. Nevertheless by this time, I had started a relationship such as it was with my daughter's mother. She was a beautiful girl, but she was an addict like me, and that has a way of subtracting from your beauty, but we loved each other, and from this dysfunctional relationship came my most precious gift, my daughter. Sandi would do anything for crack, and she had a sister, so they were both doing things that they normally would not do to support their habits.

By this time, my nephew Omar was drinking very heavy, it was cheap malt beer that he loved, he had come home from prison and he was very angry. He would drink just a little bit of beer, and it would affect him in a very weird way, he would get so violent and have these blackouts, and not remember anything that happened the night before. And Jay, well he grew up quickly, he never really had a chance to be a child, by this time he was also selling drugs. We were caught in a whirlwind, and none of us could get out. It became the place to be my grandmother's former house at 15th and Ogden Streets, and everybody wanted a piece of the action. They would set up drug corners down the street from my house, around the corner from the house, and had drug stops around the corner, anywhere and everywhere just to intercept some of the traffic that was coming to the house. Man, success breeds competition I guess, and everyone wanted some of that success, like roaches coming out of the woodworks they came, dealers from everywhere, trying to cut in on us and muscle us out of the action. Of course there was the inevitable violence that accompanied all this illegal action, shootings were up, robbery was up, hell everything was up, the money, drugs, everything was up. This one young drug dealer had set up shop right on the corner at 15th and Parrish Streets; they were trying to serve the addicts before they got to our drug house. So the boss had a quarrel with one of his workers, the worker disrespected him, and the boss left and within minutes returned with a gun and shot the teen in the groin. He hollered and screamed in pain, and I mean it was a blood curdling scream I sat up in my window and watched this young black man lying in the street screaming in pain, it was almost like watching television,. We continued to get high and still he was laying out there screaming, then the screaming starts to get on your nerves, you self-ishly wish that he would either stop screaming or just die, but he keeps on screaming. The guy no longer is a human being in my eyes; he is just someone blowing my high. The neighbors have to act as if nothing is going on, no one comes to this wounded young mans aide, finally after what seemed like forever, the police arrived and they take him to the hospital. After the police leave with the young man, we get up enough courage to walk over to where he had laid in the street, on the corner at 15th and Parrish Streets and we looked at the blood stain that was left in the street, and believe me there was a lot of blood, we found out that later that night, he had died, just like that he was gone. I doubt if the drug dealer who killed him was ever bought to justice, probably not, because I saw him riding in his Infiniti for a long time after that. He had no remorse; it was just business to him. Nevertheless, to the family of the slain young man, it was probably much more than busi-ness. It was a tragedy, another young life snuffed out before it's time, another wasted existence. From that point on, I realized that for some of our black men, it does not take much for them to shoot somebody, they would just point and shoot, and it is as simple as that!

These drug dealers were ruthless young men, whose motto was to live for today and not worry about tomorrow. They believed in fast money, fast women, fast times and fast lives. Many of these young drug dealers did not expect to live into their thirties, and many did not live into their thirties. So that is why our young black men can kill each other with such impunity because they do not value their own lives let alone someone else's. After the young guy was shot, I thought that they were going to come into the house and shoot us, so we got another gum for protection from Lamont, we were really pumped up, we thought that the showdown had come, but it did not. I will tell you something, those drug dealers did live well, the one that shot the young guy on the street corner was the first person that I saw that had an Infiniti car, it was sharp, but what price did he have to pay to get that car? How much human misery was necessary to get enough money to buy it, how many lives were ruined, how many children went hungry, how many people died? These are the questions that drug dealers do not ask themselves, perhaps it is too painful to face or perhaps they just do not care. I remember when Lamont got his new car; he personally wanted to thank each and every addict that day for making it possible for him to get that car because they supported him by buying his drugs. I have seen mothers sell there children's milk to buy drugs, I have seen parents sell their children's Christmas gifts, still wrapped up to buy drugs, oh how the children have suffered right along with the parents. The children, innocent victims of the insidious disease called drug addiction; we have to do something to save the children.

8

Guns and Drugs.

I was exposed to guns, drugs and violence in my thirties; my nephews Omar and Jay grew up in it. The guns were a big part of it. I had never shot anyone, or even held a gun in my life until that time, but I had to be educated in the way of the gun if I was going to survive. We were robbed so many times; this one time in particular stands out because Omar was upstairs listening to his rap music and it was very loud. The knock came at the door, I and Sandi were on duty selling, these two guys came in under the guise of buying drugs, they attempted to rob us, one of them punched Sandi in the face because she had the drugs, and then the other one punched me in the face. I fell forward and blacked out for a brief second. You know that it really does look like it does in the cartoons, the lights and stars spinning around your head, I was momentarily knocked out, but Sandi's screams snapped me out if it, she was struggling with one while I went after the other one, we called for Omar, but the music was too loud for him to hear us. It was like a snatch and grab and thank God they did not have a gun because they were addicts just like us or they could have really hurt us, the two robbers ran from the house, and they had a car waiting for them so they ran to the car with us in hot pursuit. They jumped into the car and the car sped of dragging Sandi as she would not let go of that pack of drugs, there was Sandi hollering and screaming as she was dragged down the street, there were the neighbors peeking out their doors and windows, it was wild. After that, Lamont gave us a 380 caliber hand-gun for protection, I felt invincible after I got the gun.

A few weeks later we were threatened by the family of a drug dealer that Omar owed money to, I would sit in the window of the house, brandishing the gun so that they could see it as they walked by as a deterrent to keep them from busting in and robbing us. Once this hooker, Kim who owed me money was coming back to the house to pay me, she was robbed by OT's cousin right on the steps of my drug house, Kim was mugged and robbed of the money that she was going to pay me. I heard her scream and looked out the window to see the young boy running with her handbag, Kim was crying because who knows how many dicks she had sucked to get that money. So even though they knew that I had the gun, the relatives of OT still busted in on us one night, it must have been about four in the morning. Some guys were downstairs selling drugs and I was upstairs sleeping when I heard a loud crash as they busted the door in. It was OT's brother; his name was Boy and his cousin. Boy and the other guy wanted the money that they thought my nephew Omar owed OT; even though OT was locked up they were there to collect. So the two of them busted into my bedroom brandishing their handguns and demanding the money, they had heard that we were making all of this money. I calmly talked to them as I knew them from the times that I worked for OT. If there was one saving grace that I had as an addict it was that I never lost my cool when someone pointed a handgun at me and meant to kill me. My nephew Omar had run up to the third floor and escaped out of the window and after he got away I showed Boy where we hid the drug money. Boy took all of the drug money and left with his cousin without hurting anyone. I was glad that no one got shot that night.

After a while, Lamont would leave the crack with us to bag up and sell. While we were bagging up the crack, I would hide rocks in my socks for getting high with later, I learned every trick in the book. As the drug business flourished more people wanted in, so Top-cat came along, he was the uncle of Omar's son, and a big drug dealer. I began to work for him also as well as Lamont and I was playing a dangerous game. I would smoke up Lamont's product and have to make it up with Top-cat's product. Nevertheless, one day Lamont found out what I was doing, he confronted Top-cat who told him the truth and we had a terrible fight. He hit me in the head with the 380 handgun. The gun went off and it shot through the floor, as he tried to shoot me in the leg, and Lamont almost shot Top-cat who was in the living room which was right underneath my bedroom. It was the first of many such beatings from drug dealers that I was willing to endure in my quest to get high. You see the drugs make you a punk, a bitch; you will take any amount of punishment to get to the bottom line, which is to get high. You no longer have any dignity, pride or self worth, the addiction takes all that from you. The addiction takes away your humanity and your courage as they are both stripped away. Nevertheless all that is left is this shell of a person, a collection of skin and bones, and this thin veneer. The total essence of a person without their soul is a collection of bones and bio-chemical components along a lot of water. That is what we are all made up of, chemicals that are worth about 97 cents, for without our souls there is nothing else there, you remain a one dimensional being, and you cannot exisit like that. The light that was my life was gone, a dim reminder of who I was and what I was. I was no longer a human being; I was more like some sort of sub-human, I less than a man, yet more than an animal, closer to the animal I believe. Because my ability to think rationally and to love and respect other human beings along with the capacity to love was gone, wiped out. Nevertheless all that was left was the degradation of my addiction, the meager existence that I now cherished. The Robert L. Glover Jr. that I and my family known and loved was gone, replaced by a beast, a monster, consumed by the demons that reside in all of us. So you don't believe in demons, how about hell, anyone doesn't believe in hell? What about the devil, any doubts that he exisit? Well, let me put your hearts at ease, yes all the above does exisit, the devil, both hell and demons. The demons live all around us, waiting for us to give them the opportunity to consume our lives. Yes, I said waiting for "US" to give them the opportunity to consume our lives. The power of evil over us, just as the power of good over us comes from within us. Its power and the direction we chose in life is a conscious decision that we make, on a daily basis, now granted it is not as cut and dry as that, but basically, there is not much more to it. Take away the mitigating factors, and we have to bear the responsibility for the actions we take, the direction our lives take, who we fuck over, and who we treat well. It is up to us, I wish I could claim some socio-economic bullshit to justify the ten years of my life that I fucked up, but I can't. I was given a base for morally correct behavior, the greatest gift that a family can instill in a child, the moral and values of his or hers parents, and family, extended or otherwise. From this knowledge I learned what was right and what was wrong, I chose to use this knowledge when it conveniently suited me, and not to use it when it also suited me. So this "book", this experience is laid on no ones shoulders but my own, I want to make this clear before I continue.

So more and more people wanted a piece of the pie, Sandi moved into the house, she slowed down her tricking, and we tried to live respectable lives as addicts, but things got progressively worse, she continued to do what women addicts do, ply their most convenient commodity, their bodies, she would do anything for drugs, I caught her getting into guys cars, man it was crazy. Sandi became ill, some sort of pelvic infection, that required her to be hospitalized at Saint Joseph's hospital. She was very ill, but she begged me for a hit, so I took her some crack and a pipe to the hospital so she could hit it in the bathroom, that is how sick we were. She would also have seizures caused by cocaine use, but she continued to get high, I could not stop her, only care for her after each seizure. Then my nephews continued their downward spirals, Omar was drinking more to drown his insecurities, you see, his mother who is my sister was never there for him. She was never there to show him right from wrong, up from down, left from right, he had to deal with these issues as best he could with the limited guidance he got from Nana, and the rest of his family, but he never got over the fact that hid mother was not there. So his black outs from drinking became more daily, and the violence consumed him. He once beat this hooker almost to death, because he thought her boyfriend stole his new sneakers. It was during a time when the electricity was off, because there were various times when the light were off. I heard him say that his sneakers were missing so he went to confront her, I was upstairs and I could hear them arguing, and then I heard him hitting something, he had a stick and it made the sickening thud like a piece of wood hitting a wall, except he was hitting her, I rushed to stop him and we had to take the girl to the hospital, and of course he remembered nothing the next day. Nevertheless that is the way it was with his blackouts.

Jay was starting to sell drugs and he becomes hooked on the street lifestyle, he grew up very quickly from this point on and all the bad things that he learned came from me. Yet we were making money and it all seemed okay. One day Worm, the loan shark came to warn us that these dealers from Sybert Street were coming to kill us. They had heard about the lucrative market that we had established and the money that we were making and of course they wanted a piece of the action. They had approached me about it and, I course said no, so the word was out that they were going to come in and shoot everyone. So we prepared ourselves it was right after Chistmas, in 1994. We boarded the windows up, and the drug dealers we worked for gave us guns to defend ourselves. They were not about to be there themselves of course so we huddled under the boarded up picture window in the living room, smoked crack, and waited to be killed, while bringing in the new year, now that was a hell of a New Year's Eve. They of course did not show up, but the tension from that point on was terrible. It became every man for him, once they came down and caught us with our pants down. They caught my nephew Jay outside, and one of the other young drug dealers named Tazz locked the door when he saw them coming, I thought for sure they were going to kill Jay, but they let him go. The violence increased exponentially. There were a group of young knuckleheads sealing drugs by then in the house, and they got there kicks by beating up addicts that messed their packs up. Messing up a pack is when you are given a certain amount of drugs to sell like there would be 25 bags of crack in a bundle, you get a percentage of the money like $25.00 dollars and whoever you were selling for got $100.00 dollars but when the count is wrong you get your ass kicked. I got caught up like that quite a few times, and was all right with it as long as I could continue to get high. So theses guys were whipping girls' asses, guys' asses' anybodies ass, and they were trying to outdo each other with the amount of reckless violence they could dole out to defenseless human beings. I saw two females get the shit beat out off them, as they saw me get the shit beat out of me, crack, makes cowards of us all. Once I got beat so bad, I couldn't walk up to the drug dealers house, he had pistol whipped me, all that shit, you name it. The other dealers that worked out of my house would sometimes beat the sellers who were all addicts if they messed up a pack. Once I saw them beat a girl in my house so bad, they threw her down the steps, punched her, threw her into a wall and threw a glass door. It turned out that she did not even mess up the pack, but they enjoyed it none the less, the drug dealers name was June, he was a real coward to beat a woman up like he did. The Drug dealers looked at addicts as being less than human, a commodity, useful only to sell their drugs to and make money. We were collateral to them, useful to support their deviant lifestyle; we allowed them to buy motorcycles, to buy cars, to purchase new clothes and homes. We made it possible for them not to have to work, to get up late, to buy all the pussy that they wanted and to eat at McDonalds whenever they felt like it. We made it possible for these drug dealers to go to the casinos whenever the mood hit them we made it possible for them to take a turn at a poker table and to play dice on the street corners for unheard of sums of money. Nevertheless, we addicts were human too, we comforted each other after we were beaten, and we came back for more. Nevertheless we took it, the beatings and the humiliation that went with it, and the torture, all of it just to get high. I would have sold my body parts if I could for a suck on that glass dick.

I began to go to the blood bank at Broad and Thompson Street. They would let you give plasma twice a week. The way it worked was that it was a procedure that took about two hours, after you waited three hours to get in, it seems like every addict in the city was there, and my cousin Chucky also gave plasma. The blood bank would take a pint of blood out of your arm, then they would take it and spin the blood in a centrifuge until the blood separated from the plasma, and then they would reinsert the whole blood back into your arm and repeat the process, this way getting a pint of plasma from you and of course it took three hours to complete. For this they would pay you fifteen dollars twice a week, with the sixth donation getting you a bonus of five extra dollars. This plasma was sold to the Red Cross for much more money than the blood bank paid us. I had to maintain a certain weight to donate because they weighed you each time you came to donate. I got so thin that I could not donate legally, so I had to put rocks in my pockets to fool the scale, when I was caught, they blackballed from there, I really missed the money, but what was really cruel was going through all of that, and then being ripped off for your money when you went to cop drugs and you find you got sold sheet rock, that happened to me a few times. Once they were selling right at 15th and Ogden streets, right behind the church, Second Pilgrim Baptist Church I had just gotten out of the blood bank; I rushed to the drug dealer. They had these fat dimes of crack and I could not wait to get there and get one, this guy was selling and I bought two of them, he seemed a little strange, he was an addict but he had the crack or so I thought. It was my bonus day at the blood bank, so that meant that I got an extra five dollars, so I had twenty that day, I rushed into my house and poured some crack into my straight shooter, lit it up and got nothing, it was sheet rock. I was so mad and because I only lived right I went back and confronted him, normally I would have taken the loss, but I really needed that wake up hit. It was just my luck that the boss was there when I got back to the selling area. I told the boss that his worker had sold me sheet rock, and of course the worker being an addict too and he tried to play me off like I was lying. Nevertheless, too many people had returned with the sheet rock, he was burning everybody and smoking up the product, the boss was furious, but that is what happens when you have an addict selling your package. He was so angry that he pulled out this gun and put it to the sellers head, he told him replace the drugs that he stole and to give me what I paid for. The guy was crying at this point, he gave me my drugs, begging the boss all of the time for his life, the boss asked me, "What should I do with this guy, should I shoot him". I was so angry that I really did not care what happened to the guy as long as I got my drugs, and besides he would not really shoot the guy if I told him too. Who was I just another addict, so I said, shoot him, and he did, the gun went off right into the guys head as I was walking away, I did not look back, or care to, I had what I needed and what I had paid for. I went right into the house and hit my drugs, fuck that guy; he tried to rip me off, good riddance I thought, man I was fucked up. That is what the drugs do to you; you do not care about anyone or anything else. They probably dumped his body somewhere; the police would find a lot of bodies around that area. I remember when this girl Tee who I knew was killed, they found her body in the lot at 15th and Poplar streets, she was selling crack for a while as well as using it, she also would trick if the money was right, Tee was beaten to a pulp, I mean beaten to the point where they could not identify her at first. Who could beat another human being so brutally, I asked myself as I watched the coroner remove Tee's lifeless body, I never got an answer to that question because the police never found her killers. Nevertheless nobody cared; it was business as usual, once the crime scene investigators and police left. I wish now that I had more humanity back then, but I was stripped naked by my addiction, a shell of a human being, existing with other people who were also shells of human beings, it was a terrible situation, but you could never imagine how we viewed the death of someone else. Even if we knew who the person it was that had gotten killed it was still, oh well, better him or her than me, it was survival of the fittest.

By this time, Sandi was pregnant with our daughter, if there was anything good that came out of theses troubled times, it was my daughter, I doubted she was mine because of the behavior of her mother, but she is mine. Also the Sybert Street gang fire bombed the house. It was the coldest day in February, and I had just got off from selling, I worked from 7 am to 7 pm, and I smelled smoke coming from the third floor. We had no water pressure in the house, I tried to but the fire out with this small bucket, filling it from the sink on the third floor bedroom, but the fire got too big. We barely made it out with our lives, and we watched as the firemen seemed to be letting the house burn down, only when the fire threatened the house next door did they put it out. As I stood there in the freezing rain, I had no idea what was being lost as I watched my late grandmother Nana's house burn down. Only now all these years later do I realize what was lost, I now know what burned with that house, the memories of my childhood, the memories of every Thanksgiving dinner, of every Christmas dinner, of every family gathering. Part of me was burning and I did not even give a damn, at that time all I saw was my way to sell drugs being taken from me, all I saw was my ability to get high going away. God forgive me but I did not see my great grandmother in the front bedroom, giving out change to go to the store. I did not see my grandfather putting on his uniform in the third floor bedroom as he prepared to go to work to as a security guard at Enon Baptist Church. I did not see my families smiling faces, our love for each other I did not see that in the fire, I just could not se that at the time. So the Red Cross came, they put us up in a hotel, the Ben Franklin Motor lodge up on 22nd and Spring Garden Streets for five days, they gave us a voucher for two-hundred and fifty dollars at J.C. Penney's, which I quickly sold to Worm so that we could buy more drugs and stay at the hotel while the drug boys put the house back together, that location was worth a lot of money and they were not about to give up their cash cow.

So we went back to the house after a few days. But I actually went back there that night by myself after the fire was put out to survey the damage. There were no third floor, just a shell of a third floor structure, and the house was frozen; I mean frozen from the water of the fire hoses, ice was everywhere. It looked surreal, like an ice cave that is how much ice was there, so I grabbed a few things and went back to the motel. A few days later we came back and got to work on the house, Lamont and Top-cat provided the lumber and the labor. A few crack addicts came to help out, so we just boarded up the steps to the third floor and turned into a two story home. Nevertheless the violence picked up right where it left off once we opened the house back up and began to sell drugs again.

One other time this guy came over, he had a reputation as a killer; he had just got out of jail, and wanted to take over our action. He came in; I was upstairs and made his way to my bedroom before I approached him. I asked him what was up. To which he replied that he was taking over the house and we would be working for him from now on. Me never having seen this man before, and not knowing or caring about any reputation, told him to "Go to Hell"! He looked at me with an incredible look of bewilderment on his face, turned and walked down the steps, and said matter of fatly. I will be back, to which I replied, 'Bullshit" So he left. I paid the incident no mind, and later that evening there was a knock on the door, now there was a whole room of guys dealing drugs at the time, it was drug dealing by committee, whoever got to the door first made the sale, and I got a piece of the action. Whether it was someone to see me about renting a room, or hitting crack in the house, the drug dealers called me as I controlled all that action. So they called me and said it was someone to see me. I come downstairs, and the killer from earlier had returned. He was one of those from up-state guys, you know when a guy is imprisoned up-state, which they send you there if you have to serve more than three years, and they tend to get big by the they get home, from weight lifting and eating good, and he was a big guy. So he says that he would like to have a word with me. Now by this time, the only furniture we had left downstairs was a couch, a television set and the dinning room table and chairs. So I sit at one end of the table and he sits at the other end. Now let me set this scene up, it was like something out of a movie, In the front room are four young boys, all tough drug dealers, two of them armed, in the dinning room are me and homeboy. He has a bag of Wendy's food, as he had just left the drive-in window. He sit's the bag down, and talking in a very calm voice begins to tell me about what respect is and how he has earned it. As he is talking, he takes the food out of the bag, and arranges it ever so nicely in front of himself, the burger in the middle, the fries on the left and the soft drink on the right, all the while talking to me about how a man like him should be respected, now I am sitting there listening, and not having a good feeling about this, when he proceeds to pull this huge gun from out of his waist. So homeboy had to go get strapped, and grab a bite to eat before he came back to see me. Now all the young tough drug dealers are sitting there on the couch with their mouths wide open, and homeboy tells them without even turning around because he is sitting with his back to them that they better not even think about pulling their guns out, so they sat on their hands. He then makes it clear to me that when he is finished eating his meal, he is going to kill me. So I look to the other guys in the living room for some help, please I say to myself, will one of these young killers shot this damn guy, but they all heed his warning and they all stay glued to the television as if nothing is happening. So with each bite he takes of the French fries, with each bite he takes of the burger, and with each sip of the soda, I see my life slowly slipping away, all the while he is assuring me it will be swift and quick. I begin to sweat now, I can see my end coming and I cannot believe that this the way my life will end, hell, I almost shit my pants by now, al the while I am looking at that huge gun sitting on the table. If only I had a gun I tell myself, I could at least defend myself, but I am unarmed. Now as he gets closer to the end of his meal, his calmness eases just a little with each bite, he becomes a little angrier, it's subtle, but noticeable. And with each bite, and with each drink, I am getting more anxious, because I am not quite ready to cash in my chips yet. Just as he puts the last bite of the burger in his mouth and reaches toward the gun, Top-cat burst into the house, now he also is armed, but being street guys they know each other, and Top-cat explains that this is his operation, mutual respect is exchanged, and the guy leaves with Top-cat. Now I turn to the young boys, especially the ones who were armed, and they assured me they were just about to blow this guys head off when Top-cat intervened. Bullshit of course, but I came this close to losing my life, it wasn't the first time and definitively wouldn't be the last time.

So homeboy came back again, a few months later. It was late at night about two or three in the morning, and he was desperate, we were open twenty four hours a day. Same set up, we had several young guys on duty, and my boy Danny, and he was supposed to be a killer. Danny would walk around the house with this shoulder holster on with his gun in it like he was a cowboy or something so homeboy came in and lined everyone up against the wall downstairs. I and Omar were off as we had finished our shifts and we were upstairs, Omar wanted to rush downstairs to stop this guy, because he had a gun, and I had to restrain him because homeboy would have killed my nephew. He told Danny, with his back to him, not to reach for the gun Danny had in his holster. And Danny froze, homeboy proceeded to take every ones pack of crack and their money and walked out the door with his back to them, he had nerve. So when the bosses arrived, the first thing they wanted to know is why didn't anyone shoot homeboy as he was going out the door, and Danny replied he didn't want to back shoot him, he wanted to see the whites of the mans eyes, everyone burst out laughing, like this shit was a western or something. Danny wanted to see the whites of his eyes before he shot him!

So we had to have some more guns for our protection, I often wondered how guns get into the streets and in the hands of criminals and I had a first hand experience of how they do. One day a friend of mine asked if we needed some guns, I said yes, and he set up an appointment with this white boy from New York City. Sure enough, a week later this white guy shows up with a suitcase, just like in the movie Taxi Driver and opens the suitcase and it is filled with guns, a 357 magnum, and a 380 and all types of guns. I go get my boss, and he buys the 357 magnum and the 380, just like that, no permits, no criminal background check, just cash on the barrel, it was real easy. I felt like a big man when my boss left me the 357 magnum, almost invincible, I dared anyone to try and rob us now. It never ceases to amaze me, even to this day how a gun can seduce you and lie to you. A gun can make you believe that you are ten feet tall, that you are invincible, that you are a great shot, that you can and will pull the trigger if you are threatened. It can give courage to the weak, provide an outlet for ones aggressions, it can create enemies, both real and imagined, and it gives you a tool to recklessly deal with any perceived threat, a gun is I now know a terrible thing.

So the violence continued as did the shootings. Once this white trick bought her date, this black guy to the house to rent a room, she came running downstairs and announced to everyone that this brother was loaded. So of course everyone in the house wanted to rob the brother, I didn't want any trouble. I tried to hold the mob back while the brother escaped, but they knocked me down, chased the guy up Ogden St. and caught him by the Met church. They were out of view by then, all I heard was the gun shot, and all of the guys that were chasing the bother to rob him are running back into the house, with the guys' money, there were about five of these nuts. They proceeded to open the bankroll, only to discover to their surprise that it was about sixty one dollar bills, wrapped by a twenty dollar bill. The police came and took the brother that they shot to the hospital, and that was the end of it, or so we thought. About a week and a half later, there was a knock on the door. I was upstairs, and one of the dealers went to answer the door. All I heard was a loud boom, the young boy named Tazz screamed as he was shot in the knee; I looked out the second floor window and could see the shooter running up Ogden Street, he was taking the same path that the mob had taken days earlier when they chased the other brother and robbed him. The shooter jumped into a waiting car and sped away. That is when pandemonium broke out in the house. All the drug dealers that were downstairs came running up the stairs almost knocking me down as I was rushing to see who had gotten shot, the fleeing drug dealers were dropping their guns, their money and their drugs, some of the drug dealers went out the back door and hopped over the fence, all the while this kid that got shot is lying in the hallway screaming holding his knee, and bleeding all over the place. The drug dealers that the wounded kid worked for arrived and took him to Saint Joseph Hospital at 16th and Girard Avenue, they rolled into the emergency ward parking lot entrance dumped him out and kept going. The kid that got shot, he was a nice kid at one time, but he tricked my girl, so I had no more use for him. Nevertheless, the shooter was the brother of the guy who they had shot and robbed ten days before, he was coming back for revenge. Nevertheless he shot the kid in the same place his brother got shot, in the knee. The drug dealer who got shot was crippled for life, he still walks with a limp and wears a knee brace, but everything returned to normal within an hour of the shooting and we were open for business again selling drugs as if nothing had happened. No one really cared about the guy Tazz that got shot; I think that we all learned a lesson from that, the lesson being that every addict has a family and people who care about them, people who will retaliate when the addict in their family is harmed. Nevertheless, the kid Tazz who got shot, well he was forgotten about as soon as he was disposed of at the hospital, he was just another replaceable part in the machine, no one could care less, we just carried on.

9

The End at Fifteenth Street.

As Sandi became pregnant, we did began to slow down our drug use, we began to eat better, we tried to live a little more respectable, hell I even believed she slowed down her extra activity if you know what I mean, but I can never be sure of that. Nevertheless things were still progressing to the point of no return. Top-cat began to take my profits from the drug sales and bank it for me, he took me shopping for new clothes, he bought a new mattress and box spring for me, and we needed a refrigerator and he bought that also with my money, but it was about to take a turn for the worst. We always accepted the fact that we needed guns to play this game, and we had a variety to choose from, but one gun, a twenty five caliber automatic was of special concern. This particular gun had belonged to the kid Tazz that was shot some time earlier, after he was shot the gun passed on to me, I had it for protection, it was light, and easy to conceal, and it had just enough fire power to deter anyone from robbing me. It looked like a toy actually. I had it in my coat pocket this one particular day. I had just purchased everything this addict had. You see drug addicts have this way of fooling themselves, whether it is the first of the month when the SSI checks come out or bi-weekly when welfare checks came out. We always intend to do the right thing. We make plans, we map out our course, what bills we are going to pay, we make a shopping list, and we are going to buy food. We do all these things, with good intentions, until the money gets in our hands, then all these good intentions go out the window, that first hit of crack destroys all the best laid plans of mice and men. So this guy had bought himself all new gear, new

Timberlands, new down coat, the works, then he came to get high at my house, now he completed the first part of his plans he did buy something new to wear, but he wore them to the hit house, and when the money is gone, you sell whatever is left, your shoes, your clothes and your body if need be, whatever someone else will pay for, you sell it. So geuss who ended up with all this guys new gear, me! So here I am, standing on the porch with some of the drug dealers, with this twenty five caliber gun in my pocket of the new down coat, and the safety is off, as I go to pull the gun out of my pocket, it went off, blowing a hole in my new coat, passing through my thigh, and ricocheting of the cement porch and almost hitting everyone that was standing there. At that point I should have known that guns were bad news, but I kept it the gun, it gave me a sense of power, and that gun would change everything, for me, my nephew Omar and for one man's family forever. What I am about to write about is the most painful thing that happened to me while under the influence of drugs. I make now bones about the right and the wrong of it, I merely must put this down on paper, to help heal myself, and all who were involved, I let you the reader is the judge. This particular day started like all others, it started with me driven by the need to get high, I always woke up with the cravings, I went to bed with the cravings, the monkey is always there, and it was a part of me. We had an uneventful day up to that point, but there was one guy who had started to come around. He was in a shelter with his family waiting for housing because of you guessed it, his drug addiction. He was a nice guy, and we talked a lot, about his dreams for his family, his hoping to beat his addiction, and his shame and remorse for what he had put his family through.

He, like most addicts meant well, but every time he and his wife got food stamps or welfare money for those children, the beast would take over, and he would spend the money, and those good intentions that we talked about earlier went right out the window. So we would talk about his remorse after the fact, because I helped him smoke it up I would listen, hell I had been there before myself. So this particular day, he was there all day, it must have been check day for him, and he was spending, and we were all having as good a time as addicts can have until I ran out of drugs. I had to go get more so I had to leave the gun with Omar; he had a bad habit of pointing guns at people and pulling the trigger, with no bullet in the gun. Omar had been drinking all day it was his way to relieve his anger and frustrations, and most of all; he meant no harm to anyone. I mean what he was doing was wrong, but Omar was not a bad person, he just had bad luck. So I give him the 22 handgun and tell him I am going to get more drugs, he is to hold on to the handgun until I get back. The guy comes to the front door to give me his money so that I could get more, and as I am leaving, I tell him to go back into the house, just then Omar comes down the steps, it was pretty loud and it was a house full of people, I here one of the girls in the hose say, ' No Omar, don't", then the gun goes off, and the guy fall out of the doorway at my feet onto the porch, with this small hole in his head. The hole is so small it looks like a dot surrounded by a little bit of blood, he has this surprised look on his face, and his mouth was formed such as if he was saying no, it was a moment frozen in time. Sandi and I looked at each other, Omar came out the house and said that he didn't mean to do it; he was very drunk, threw the gun away and fled into the night. I did not know what to do, so I went to my boss, and he said that he would take care of it. He paid some addicts to put the guys' body across the street, and we called the police and reported the shooting, hoping that they would find him. They didn't, we called five times they drove by five times, it was very cold, and by morning he was frozen solid.

The police finally found him by morning and they kicked my front door in. You know the strange thing about this whole incident, was they way we carried on all night, continuing to sell and use drugs as we detached ourselves from the situation. A human being was dying or dead. Nevertheless, we carried on like nothing happened, that is the most painful part of this, is the remembering, and dealing with feelings and emotions that I did not want to and sometimes still do not want to deal with. I cannot imagine how some of these young black thugs can kill people over and over without any remorse. Is it because they are psychologically incapable of feelings? Or is it some sort of pathological sickness that allows them to detach themselves for the taking of a human life? Was I made sicker from my addiction than I thought that I was, was I now pathologically inhuman? I guess that I was, but I do know now that this haunts me every waking moment of everyday. Then I guess that we all were like inhuman animals, we didn't care about anything. No remorse, no feelings no nothing. We did not care that a mother had lost her son, a sister had lost her brother, a wife had lost her husband, and children had lost their father, all that was important at the time was the crack, the next hit.

So the police kicked the front door in and took everyone who was in the house to the Roundhouse, there were four of us in the house at the time; they did not take Sandi because she was pregnant. So they took the three of us down to the Roundhouse, homicide division. Imagine how naïve I was to think that I could keep something as big as a murder hidden from the police, to protect my nephew. Hell they knew the whole story by the time we got to the police station, the whores and other drug addicts in the neighborhood had told the police what happened but they still needed me to cooperate and tell them what they already knew to. Every whore in the neighborhood was taken downtown until they talked, they told the police who did the shooting and where he lived, and so I was fighting a losing battle on that one. My second experience with the police was not any more pleasant than the first one. They handcuffed me to a chair, I was in this interrogation room for more than sixteen hours, they would not let me eat anything or drink anything, there was a little physical action, you know they hit me more than a few times, but I still tied to hold out, you know for my nephew Omar who was family. At the end of the day, after being beaten and not given food or water, I said what they wanted to hear, and signed a document to that effect, I felt bad for my nephew, but had no choice, the homicide detectives broke me. They broke me and I am not ashamed to admit it, and anyone who thinks that they are brave enough to hold out when being interrogated by the police is fooling him or herself, they have ways to make you talk, they are experts. The food deprivation, sleep deprivation, water deprivation it was all effective. The detectives took us back to the house; where there was a hero's welcome for me from the drug dealers, and some crack to smoke too. I know they had tricked my girl while I was downtown, but at this point I really did not care.

So the manhunt was on for my nephew Omar, the police put out an all points bulletin on Omar with his description. He had no memory of what he had done because he was so drunk, he surely blacked out afterward. He would call on the phone and I felt so bad that he was on the run, because to him, he did not do anything wrong. Then came the terrible aftermath of the crime, the murder victim left behind, a family, a wife, children, brothers and sisters, and they had to deal with this awful event, even as we did not want to. The family would come to the lot across the street from our drug house where the police found the body of their loved one, and the family would stare at the house, they knew that we were in the house, then they would place flowers on the spot where they found him, and all the time as I peeped out the window, high as hell, and scared as hell. You see every addict that you see out in the street, has someone to remember him or her, they have some family member, some child some brother, some parent, no one is born to be an addict, at some time his or her life was full of promise. They were the "one" in someone's eyes, the twinkle, the sparkle that lit up parent's eyes when they looked at them, and then, all of it taken away, by this unforgiving bastard, this mother-fucker that is this addiction, which is an equal opportunity enslaver. It does not care where you come from, who you come from, how you came from. It is the walking death, which makes slaves out of human beings. There is nothing glorious about that life, those who live it are cursed, and many do not recover. So like I said the manhunt for my nephew was on. There was a three page write up in the Philadelphia Inquirer, where they tried to make my nephew into some sort of super drug kingpin, and that he had killed the man over money, they where so wrong and so far from the truth. It was a senseless accident, and that is all it was, I know because I was there. So Omar ran, the police kept coming to the house, searching for him, always while we were trying to get high, man I hated that, until weeks later this same white detective came by to tell me that they caught Omar. Omar really did not remember pulling that trigger after he sobered up from the alcohol; he was apprehended trying to get his welfare check at the 321 center on Broad and Girard Avenue. So after the police apprehended Omar, that meant no more visits from the police and things could get back to normal, we could continue to destroy our lives without interference, which we did!

The house had reached its peak around this time, and we were officially labeled as a public nuisance by the city of Philadelphia. This was also the time when they were shooting the movie "12 Monkeys", with Bruce Willis in the Met church at Broad and Popular Sts.; this movie also had Brad Pitt in it. We were so pissed off because while they were filming the movie and they had all types of Hollywood people there, and all types of police for their protection, right in our line of business. I don't have to tell you that business dropped off after that, and stayed dropped off until they finished the movie, or the part they were shooting at the Met. The Met, always there, me and the Met have always had a history, before I started smoking crack, I was selling weed at my grandmothers house, I was still living a life of some normalcy, and had money galore, I was working at University of Pennsylvania, at the Computer Connection, and making gobs of money. I had bought a Volvo, always loved Volvos even though I couldn't drive, and to make matters worse, it was a stick shift. So I paid my friend Kevin to drive it home to my grandmothers house, and one day, during the nineteen eighty four Olympics, me and my cousin Chucky were getting high and drinking beer. At this point the decided that I was ready for my first driving lesson, we were both pretty on, so off we went to drive my new car, we were going around the block as he explained the fundamentals of driving a stick shift, relaxing and talking when I noticed, as did he that the corner was coming real fast he hollered hit the clutch, he meant hit the break, the car took off and rammed right into the Met wall, the Volvo emblem is still embedded in the wall, that's how fast we were going. I had to go to the hospital right after the car crash, my cousin Chuckey was knocked unconscious and my chin hit the steering wheel. The impact of me hitting the steering wheel caused a huge gash on my chin, blood was spurting everywhere and all I could think of was cussing my cousin Chuckey out, and him being unconscious he did not hear anything that I said to him. Nevertheless I had to go to

Saint Joseph's hospital and get my chin stitched up, it was so big afterward that I looked like a pelican and it hurt like crazy. So I paid a guy to tow my car, it was totaled but he still told me he could fix it, he lied he was just trying to rip me off.

So we were a public nuisance and the people were tired of the crime that came with it, three shootings and then a murder, so on the same day that Timothy Mcvie bombed the federal building in Oklahoma, we were put out of our house. The sheriffs came with the police, and License and Inspections with a truck and work crew to board up the house. We were given 15 minutes to get ourselves together and to take what we could carry out of the house with us, they took my new refrigerator, my new bed and boarded the house up, and we left with the clothes on out back, a radio and some food. We went to Top-cat to get whatever money he was holding for me, and it was just a few hundred dollars. So we got a room at the Blue Horizon, a local whore house on Popular and 15th sts. We stayed there for a few days until our money ran out, me and Sandi. I remember the devastation playing out on the television, at the Federal Building in Oklahoma as we watched on Top-cats mother s television, while we waited for him to get home. I remember watching the firemen and rescue workers bringing out the bodies of the little children from the daycare that was in the federal building, and that one scene that will forever be remembered is the one of the rescue worker carrying out the little girls' bloody body. You sort of remember where you were doing moments of crisis. I remember where I was, in school when they shot the president, J.F.K. I was in grade school at the time, we watched on TV in our classroom, as teachers were crying, I was too young to understand, but you have to remember, J.F.K. got shot on the 22nd of November, and my birthday was on the 28th, and my sister Robin's birthday was on the 25th, so all I remember was how his assasination ruined my birthday. I remember where I was when they killed Dr. Martin Luther King Jr. I was home when the word came out over the television that Dr. King was dead, we didn't dare go out, as Philadelphia was set ablaze, in a rampage of violence and looting. The whole country went up in smoke that night as black people took out their rage on their own neighborhoods in an orgy of violence, death and destruction. I remember where I was when Malcolm X got assassinated, just as I remember where I was when I woke up and Cassius Clay had won the heavyweight championship of the world. I remember where I was when they assassinated R.F.K., I was on my class trip, to New York of all places, it had been planned months earlier, and we went to a play and had dinner, R.F.K., being the senator from New York at the time, his assasination closed down the whole city, it was like a ghost town, some class trip that turned out to be.

And now I remember where I was when Timothy McVie bombed the federal building, this event will forever be linked to me; I was high when that happened. I have lived and seen some terrible things while I was high. It seemed surreal to us, so unimportant at the time, the hell with those people I thought, we were homeless, and what was much more importance, and we had no way to support our habit, because we had no more drug house to sell drugs from. So we decided to stop smoking Sandi and I, we met one of Sandi's friend, and she took us to a place she had rented in the past, but still had the keys, so we stayed there without the landlords consent. This apartment was on Broad Street, right across the street from Progress Plaza, and we had to be very careful when we left, one person always had to stay behind, so we would get locked out, and we had to be very quiet during the day. I felt like I was in the movie The Diary of Ann Frank, like we were hiding from the Nazi's or something. Nevertheless we actually did do better, I was making money washing cars, and there was an old peach tree that I would get peaches from so we actually started to eat healthy, we slept and waited for the baby to be born

10

The Birth of My Daughter.

Soon we were discovered by the landlord and put out of the apartment, so homeless and without a place to go we went to the hospital and tried to get in but the contractions were not close enough, so we left and went to a playground at 12th and Brown Streets. Sandi stared to swing on the swing higher and higher I pushed her, she was sure that this would start the process, so she swung until she started to have contractions. She was admitted, and our daughter was born hours later. I was in the delivery room, and will never forget when she came popping out, like she was greased on a chute or something, it was one of the happiest days off my life. I now had a daughter and I was forty years old, and I did not have a clue that my life was about to change forever. My mother and sisters came to the hospital to greet little Sandra, babies have a way of healing families, of drawing them closer together especially after they have grew apart. I wanted to name her after my mother, and Sandi wanted to name her after herself, so she won, and I gave little Sandra my mothers first name for her middle name, Mozell, I thought that was fitting, and it was an honor well deserved. I stayed in the hospital as long as I could, sleeping on the floor until they told me I had to leave, being homeless, with nowhere to go and being a new father was scary, but once again my family stepped in and offered me a haven for my daughter and girlfriend. We went to stay at my late grandmother Mom-mom's house, where my nephew and brother where staying. Now my nephew was working, as was my brother, and he was battling his own addiction problems, not the best place to be, but we had no where to go and we were thankful. At first for our daughters' sake we tried to stay clean. We made a vow, and a pact between us, Sandi and me that we would do no more drugs, there were many such pacts made like this throughout our addiction. And for a while it worked, but you can only get clean for yourself, not for anyone else. In the meantime, while we were clean I got a job working for the old Clover chain, I was on the shelf stocking unit, and while I was at work, Sandi and my brother were getting high together, it started when Sandi's sister Lynn came over to get her hair fixed, and I went to go to Murray's to get some food with the money, all our clean time went out the window, for if Sandi was getting high I certainly was going to.

So while working at Clover my addiction kicked back in, I went from model worker to drug up worker, I began to steal from the store, all kinds of merchandise, game gears, video games and compact disk, whatever was not nailed down. I would get paid from my job and still not have carfare to get to work. I would catch the sixty one buses every morning and explain to the driver that I forgot my tokens that worked for a while until he got tired of that story then I was forced to walk to work. My sister Sharon was a manager at Clover, she warned me that they were watching me but I had to have it, it did not matter to me I thought that I was slicker than the security people at the store were. So as I was leaving work one day with my bag full of stolen merchandise, I was stopped by security, I broke away and ran, they chased me all through center city, and the police caught me in China-town. I was taken to the police station, once more, released on my own recognizance, and I went home embarrassed. I know my sister Sharon was embarrassed; she still had to work there, so here I was once again without a job, back on welfare and loving it, but not really though. Nevertheless as it got worst for me it got worst for my daughter. About this time, my younger brother Donald came home from prison. He was there on a drug charge. He had been like most of us, lost in this world, in it and off it. He had been married, divorced. Sent to a re-hab in Wilkes-Barrie Pa., came home and got high at my brothers house, then got locked up in New Jersey, trying to bring drugs in from New York. When we were little, there were always ten of us, siblings. Four sisters and six boys, that always remained a constant. When you are small like that, you tend not to think of life and death; you have your whole life ahead of you. You don't think of the future, what you might become, or how you might fuck you life up, you only imagine that as a family you will always be together.

11

The Death of My Brother Donald.

You think you are invincible when you are young, oh people live and people die all around you, sometimes your friends, sometimes your older relatives, and you almost expect the elderly in your family to die but you think that you and your siblings will always be together. When you are young, you think of death in terms of something that will come a long time away, as a matter of fact, you don't think of death at all. You think of living forever, just you and your brothers and sisters, you recall all of the times that you shared, both good and bad. I remember my brother Donald when we worked on the railroad together, my brother William got us the job. We were working at night and we were repairing the tracks for Con-rail, it was very dangerous work, but Donald always kept up our spirits with laughter and clowning, and that's how he was, always joking. I also remember the time when he had to be rushed to the hospital because of a scat car that he got for Christmas was broken and he injured himself by falling on it, he could not have been more than ten years old. I remember his smile; I remember that he just wanted to live like all of us I guess. I will never forget the times we spent together, the trips to the swimming pool at fifth and Allegheny at the recreation center there.

I will never forget the times we spent gathering wild blackberries along the train tracks on Seventeenth Street and Indiana Avenue, and the wonderful blackberry cobbler that my mother would make for the family as a reward for our efforts. That blackberry cobbler was known throughout the neighborhood, and when my mother would bake it the smell would fill the block of Toronto Street and every kid would show up at my house for a taste. I will remember how smart he looked in his Cub Scout uniform, and how he attended the Cub Scout meetings religiously. I will never forget the great times we had at Hershey Park, the rides we shared on the roller coaster and the times we spent in the arcade there. I will always remember when my father would give us haircuts to save money on the barbershop bill. Do not forget that there were six boys, so we had to save money whenever we could and this particular time my dad had messed up Donald's head, I mean he butchered the poor boy, Donald was so mad that he said our dad had made him look like a fucking Frankenstein, it was so funny. I will never forget his struggle to overcome substance abuse and how he finally triumphed. I will remember his marriage to Nanette and the beautiful children that came from that union; you remember all of the things that happen when you are young, and as you get older. I will always remember his marriage ceremony and how handsome he looked in his tuxedo. How he had his whole life ahead of him, it was something to see.

When someone dies, it is a horrible reality to face the mortality of your siblings and yourself, it forces you to finally see that you are not immortal. For the parents to bury a child is as horrible as they say it is. Well, my brother Donald had came home from jail, he almost died in there as they had to remove one of his lungs, but it seemed that they removed the malcontent part of him, don't get me wrong, he was never a bad guy, or an evil guy, but just like all of us growing up in that environment he was easily seduced by the dark side. So when he came home this time he was different, he was at peace with himself, the best person he had ever been. He went to the Million Man march in Washington D.C., and came back from that experience determined to make it, and be a better father to his children, and to make a difference in his community. He never got the chance. He was going to me his fiancée, it was raining, and he was walking to meet her, on Glenwood Avenue, he was crossing the street, when he was struck by a speeding car, being driven by a minor who had stolen the car, and he was hit by the police car that was chasing the kid up a one way street the wrong way. He was killed instantly. I remember my sister Sharon calling me on the phone, to tell me he was dead, I couldn't believe it. I rushed to her house. We had to go over my brother Williams's house to tell hi our brother was dead, as we were driving we had to pass the crime scene, there were people milling about, and they had him laying there, with a sheet coving him. I begged for them to move him, a policeman came up to me, explained that this was a murder scene, and they could not move him yet, he then gave me Donald's umbrella, all that was left of him. I clutched that Umbrella to me, I could feel him; we went back to the house and waited for the police to come and officially report the crime. The police did, and it was as if the pain was real all over again. We were caught off guard, we could not even bury him because we could not afford it, we had to struggle to put him to rest, and the funeral was beautiful. The choir from my sister Sharon's church performed and they sung a song "IN HIS WELL, WITH MY SOUL", I was shaken, and our lives were never the same.

My brother was dead; and there were no longer ten of us. Because we had no insurance for him we had him cremated, his remains lie in a beautiful urn that remains in my mother's possession, I cry every time I think of him. It is true I geuss, that God only take you when you are at your best, well, he was at his best. The best he had ever been, then he was taken from us before was had a chance to enjoy him, I took God to task for that, then I understood, his journey was over, his pain was gone, and Donald had paid his debt, now it was time for him to go home. We did not want him to go, for our own selfish reasons; we never want our loved ones to go. Nevertheless, there is a greater glory out there for all of us, and we shall all see it one day, only when we are at out best, at our best, I love Donald, and will always miss him dearly. I was forty years old when he died, but at least he got to meet my daughter Sandra, held her at a family cookout the summer before he was killed. I am grateful for that; he took a piece of her to heaven with him. Donald left behind two sons, Donald JR. and his brother Dominique.

My Nephew Omar:

Also around this time, I was subpoenaed to appear in court as a witness for the prosecution against my nephew Omar, for killing the guy he killed. I was on my way down to the Criminal Justice Center, when I saw them bringing the prisoners from State Road, where the jails are located. I remembered my ride on that bus, and I saw Omar on the bus, he looked so lost almost like he did not know what was happening. Then once I was inside the courtroom, I had to face the murdered man's family; they were there in full force. His widow, his sister and brother, they looked at me with hate in their eyes and heart. Then they bought my nephew Omar in, and the trial started. The only good that came from that trial was that I was able to convey to the jury and to the judge the terrible tragic events that had happened that day. That it was not a crime of revenge, or not directly tied to drugs it was just a terrible accident, and that Omar did not know what he was doing, and how drunk he was, I believe my testimony saved his life. The thing that I will always remember about that is the way Omar looked at me, he of course had no recollection of what he was accused of, so I had to fill in the blanks, I felt like I was betraying him, but they gave me no choice. So he was sentenced to 7 1/2 to 13 years but his life was spared, and we have never talked since then. He never got to see his cousin, my daughter Sandra, he used to rub Sandi's tummy while she was pregnant, while proclaiming this is my cousin in there and we better take care of her. Omar's son had to grow up without a father, the same way Omar did, so it was the continuation of abandonment in the black community, the perpetuation of the absence of role models for black males, and the continued destruction of blacks as a people, thru the disenfranchising of boys from their fathers. It had to face the murdered man's family in the hallway outside the courtroom while the court was in recess, the only thing good is that it kept me clean for a while, but after a while I sunk back into my old habits. Sandi and I began smoking up the welfare money, we began to borrow money from a loan shark name Elaine, and you know twenty for forty. And life went out of control again. My mother called the Department of

Human Services on us, and they came out to investigate us, we slipped past but barely. Now here's how I know that there is a God, and how powerful he is, even though we subjected our daughter to our drug use, she is normal, even though her mother used drugs while carrying her, she is normal, it is as if God wrapped that baby in his hand, and protected her from all the evil that we exposed her to, he must have great plans for little Sandra, he is all powerful, he is God! It was not anything we did; we were trying to destroy ourselves.

I stole my nephews' compact disks, and sold them to anyone who would buy them, for money to buy drugs with, a favorite customer was the girl that lived across the street, and she bought most of them. I got a job with the Internal Revenue Service, processing tax returns, at night, this proved to be my undoing. While working there, I stole a check, some taxpayer had sent in their payment by check, and a blank check was sent in with the good check, so I pocketed the check. I held on to it for many weeks, until I hatched a scheme with the loan shark Elaine to cash it in her bank account. Well I don't have to tell you how that turned out. The check was sent back, they investigated, and the trail led back to me. I was shocked when it did, but it took three years to finally up to catch me, I was living in my brothers' house at the time. How that happened was my mom finally had enough of Sandi and I getting high, she told us to go get help, my sister took our daughter, little Sandra, and would have her for the next four years while the insanity of my addiction continued. I had borrowed some money from a loan shark and could not pay it back and my mother found out about it. So Sandi and I both went to this program called Phoenix Two. It was one of those tough love programs run by former addicts that mean well, but are not trained to conduct therapy or licensed to run programs, I stayed until I got my check, and left. They had us sweeping out vacant lots in the neighborhood, we would march to church every Sunday, and you had to sleep six people in a small bedroom. It reminded me of growing up in Toronto Street all over again, except these were grown men in a fourteen by fourteen room. They only had one bathtub at the recovery house, so you were assigned a bath day for an hour once a week and if you missed your bath day you were out of luck. They also had a Sunday therapy meeting where you had to sit on a milk crate and everyone would berate you, you had to accept anything and everything that they said about you. Also they took your food stamps and that is how you ate, they cooked there horrible meals, once they took this hard rice that was left over form dinner the night before and put it into the eggs the next morning to make omelets, the rice was hard as hell. We ate chicken backs that were fried for dinner, man it was horrible, but at least they were staying clean, it was just not for me, so I made plans to leave. I told them that I had found religion, and that it would save me, I said nothing about God, just religion. Like most people I mistook religion for the belief in God. The goal was to get Sandi and go get little Sandra from my sister Vicky, and start over fresh. You would not believe what happened when I arrived at the house where Sandi was staying, they would not let me see her, and she was at that point already turned out by a lesbian named Helen who ran the house, so I went to my brothers' house, spent my food stamps and cash and got high. Nevertheless just when I thought it could not get any worse, guess what, it did. So began the next three years of my living hell on 10th street.

I had been going to my Brother William's house all through my addiction, and now I was living there full time. His house was once a nice home but now had been turned in the hit house of the neighborhood. I remember when he bought that house, him and his then girlfriend Beverly; she was the mother of his children. He was so proud of his home, this was before his addiction kicked in, back then, and he was just another normal hard working parent trying to raise his family. I remember when his oldest son, Jay, accidentally set the house on fire, he was playing with matches, and he was very young. I remember how the whole family, me included rushed to his house after the fire, and I remember how he cried, we assured him that we would help him put the house back in order, and we did, but that seemed a long time ago. Since that time, his house had become something else, something insidious, and something evil. Every addict in the neighborhood knew Ghost, that's what they called my brother William from the gang war days, when he belonged to a gang. The gang was 15th and Clearfield streets, a very minor gang in the scheme of things. Nevertheless William knew all of the drug addicts and everyone would come there to get high, especially the white addicts from the suburbs. The under-cover addicts, they would show up with gobs of money, spend out, and then hang around begging for hits of crack. They would then sell their jewelry, or they would max out their credit cards, or we would ride to the gas station and use the gas card to buy cartons of cigarettes. Then we would take the cigarettes to the store and sell them, or my brother would purchase the cigarettes for a hit or two of crack. Also in the house was my brother's girlfriend Tiny, as ruthless an addict as I ever seen, like most addicts the drugs came first for her, the drugs came before her kids, before her piece of mind, and before her sanity. They would fight all the time over the drugs, the two of them would fight over the last hit, the first hit and the hit in between. I was played off against her by my brother William, so she really did not like me some-times, we were competing for the same hit of crack, and my brother was a master at getting people does anything for a hit.

Then there were the people who were there spending their pay-checks, spending the money that they were supposed to take home to their families. They would be paranoid as can be, looking out the win-dow or peeping from the blinds, watching for their wives to come and get them because they were neglecting their children and spending the rent money, the grocery money, and the clothing money. Once Zandy, who was a friend that I got high with spent the money that he was sup-posed to take to a lawyer to stop a foreclosure on his house, instead of doing that, we smoked the money up and they ended up loosing their house, his wife and him, man that shit was crazy.

Another time this guy had been over my Brother William's house, we were getting high, it was a Friday night and he spent up his two weeks paycheck. It was early Saturday morning; the money had run out, the credit had run out, the only thing that did not run out was our insanity, our desire to get high. So we are sitting there and trying to come up with a scheme and a plan to get some money when the guy says that he needs ride to his house to get something to sell. My brother who had a piece of a car told me to drive the guy home. After driving Tony home I parked the car and waited, he snuck back into the house and minutes later came out with a case of Similac milk that was for his newborn baby. We took it to a stop and go Sunoco gas station and the guy bought it for 25 dollars, it was worth about sixty dollars. That little bit of money did not last long, so after it was gone, he said to take him back to his house, which I did, once again I parked and waited. As I sat there, I hoped that he could come through again; sadly I cared nothing about his baby who had no formula to drink because I just wanted to keep getting high. After a few moments that seemed like an eternity, I heard a noise, it was so quiet that any noise stood out that time of the morning, it had to be about four in the morning. I tried to focus on where the sounds were coming from, then Tony appeared, he was running down the street caring this heavy item, and as he got closer, I could see that it was a television set, it must have been a 25 inch television set. As he approached the car, I could see that he was not alone, the person that was screaming was his wife, and she was running behind him telling him to bring the television set back into the house. His wife was dressed in her bathrobe, as if he woke her up from her sleep and that is all she could find to put on. She was screaming for someone to call the police, she had a little baseball bat, the kind that they gave out to the first five hundred children at a Philadelphia Phillies baseball game. His wife was hitting the shit out of him with the baseball bat, all the while screaming for the police and for her husband Tony to return to sanity and return the television set. She screamed that his children would not have a television set to watch; all the while Tony is getting closer and closer with the television set. Tony is taking some hellacious hits from the baseball bat from his wife; she is hitting him as if she is trying to drive the demon of addiction from his body. She is hitting him for all of the disappointments that his addiction has caused her and their family; she is hitting him for spending the paycheck, for stealing the baby's formula, for stealing the television set and for being a drug addict. Tony yells to me to open the car door so that he can put the television set into the back seat of the car. I open the door and he gently places the television set down, all the while his wife is hitting him with everything that she has, as tears of defeat roll down her cheeks. Tony gets in the car and before I can pull off, she hits him a few more times through the open car window. Nevertheless as we pulled off, I could see his wife crying in the middle of the street, dressed in her bathrobe, with no television to watch anymore. As for Tony, he was bleeding from the beating he took, but he did not care we had accomplished our mission, when we got back to my brothers house, we took the television set down to the badlands at eighth and Tioga streets, a notorious Hispanic area were they sold drugs and were open all night. I think that we may have gotten about thirty five dollars for that television set, and when we smoked that up, the party was really over, no more money, nothing else to sell, this party was over. Not only for us, but for this poor guy Tony, he had to eventually go home and face the music, he had to eventually go home and face his hungry children and a baby that had no formula to drink and now they also had no television set to watch either. He had to eventually go home and face his disappointed wife, and his disappointed life, he eventually had to face the fact that he was a no good drug addict.

I lived in the middle bedroom at my brother Williams's house, and the ceiling leaked like crazy when it rained and it was cold as hell in the winter time. The room also had no window; it had only a sheet of plastic covering it, meanwhile, my brother kept the front bedroom in tip top shape. They had a kerosene heater, a microwave oven to cook in, and the roof didn't leak yet in their bedroom. So they were warm, cozy and dry, while I froze to death. My brother charged me rent everyday about ten dollars, which meant I had to go out and hustle it up, I tried several ways to earn money but found the best way. Have you ever seen these people pushing shopping carts down the street? Well the carts are not filled with groceries, but metal like aluminum cans and copper pipes. This is what I became to support my habit, a shopping cart man, and it began the great spiral down to the most degradation I had ever known in my life, only at the time I didn't know it!

12

A Shopping Cart Is More than Just a Shopping Cart;

As I began to settle in to life with my brother William, I needed a better solution to the age old addict's problem, where to get money to support my addiction. This is a problem that has plagued addicts since the first junkie. I could not sell my body, the thought of that was disgusting. Besides the female addicts had the prostitution wrapped up, not that there were not men out there doing that too, something for everyone I guess, but that was not for me. Nevertheless, in between checks, I needed a gimmick, and I found one. When I was clean, sober and "normal", I would see these guys pushing these shopping carts. Some were filled to the brim with aluminum and other metals; some were filled with old clothes and rags depending on the severity of the mental illness of the person pushing the shopping cart. And I used to get so pissed of at these bums for blocking the street because they were in the way. I would blow my horn angrily, and they would continue on their way, they would be impassive to all around them. I would wonder how in the hell anybody could get like that, well I was about to find out. My career as a shopping cart man started innocently enough. I started by picking up aluminum cans one day. Just as a way to make enough money to buy something to eat, some cookies, or the junkies meal which is a couple of "Little Debbie's" cakes, so I would fill a couple of plastic bags with these aluminum cans, and take them to the salvage yard, it was owned by Nick, and he would give me the going rate for a pound of aluminum. He would always tell me, "Papa, you got to do better than this to make some money", and he was right. I never thought that I would or could make enough to support my habit, but I found that I could. I hooked up with some seasoned pros, these were other junkies who were in the metals game for a minute, and they showed me the ropes. You have to get a shopping cart which I did. Then I had to learn what metals were valuable. At first I was picking up anything, and Nick would say, "Papa, you got to do better than this", so I learned, and I became so good that it was scary, and that is what helped to ruin my life for the next three years. When you came into Nick's with a lot of aluminum or copper, he would holler, "What a load, bring it right over here papa". I longed to hear him say that, because that meant that I had made a lot of money and that I would smoke very well that day. It would be so hot in the summertime that we would pick up soda bottles that still had some soda in them and drink it, or I would go to the schools around lunchtime and get the aluminum trays that the lunch was served on out of the trash, many I would turn into Nick's, but some still had food in the trays and I would take them home and eat them later, like hotdogs and beans, or potato puffs and Salisbury steak, that was my meal for the day, which meant that I did not have to starve that night.

To some people the shopping cart is an inanimate object, a tool to be used in supermarkets and department stores, the shopping cart something familiar and identifiable. Then to a small segment of our society, the shopping cart is much more than that, it is a friend and a companion a thing that is alive, this is how I felt about my shopping cart, it was my friend, my companion and my partner in crime. I was taken under the wings of some very good master shopping cart men, they were heroin addicts and they could steal the eyes from a blind man, I mean they were that good. They taught me that the best time to get out there and rob people was around four in the morning when they were asleep, that way you could slip into their yards or into that abandoned house next door and strip the copper clean before anyone was the wiser. They called it "Looking for work", these old guys who showed me the ropes, everybody else called it stealing; I guess that it is all how you look at it. Nevertheless, the thing is that no matter what your drug of choice was, you were on a mission, and this mission had to be completed on a daily basis. I can say that I learned from the best, and they were the best that ever did it. With the help of my shopping cart, I learned to be a master thief. I would go around to people's backyards in the dead of night and steal what they had, period, I was a thief. I would steal their aluminum screen doors; I would steal their copper out of their basements when their houses were vacant. I am sure many of you have awakened to find your old familiar front or back screen door missing, I got you. Some addicts chained their shopping carts to telephone poles, some addicts hid them on their porches, me I hid my in an old lot near 10th and Ontario Streets. In the lot there was a dead Doberman Pincher that was decaying and smelling, but that dead dog protected my shopping cart just as if it were alive, he was my watch dog. No one would dare go back there with this dead dog smelling up the place, I finally got used to the smell of decaying flesh, just to protect my shopping cart. We would steal steel grates from the windows of houses and sell them to an antique dealer I knew, he would in turn sell them to dealers in the south, they were worth a lot of money.

The Beginning of the End

The beginning of the end started the day I went to live with my brother, I thought we had a bad drug house at 850 N. 15th street, but we had nothing on my brother. I lived in a room in which I had an electric heater, which he regulated when I could use it. I was awakened at all times of the night, so that he could rent out the room for prostitution. Once a black guy and a Hispanic guy came to rent my room one night so I was forced to get out of bed, I was sitting in my brothers room when the black guy called out to me, he wanted me to get some more crack cocaine for the both of them so I went and copped the crack cocaine, when I got back he told me to come in and when I did both the black guy and the Hispanic guy were butt naked, apparently they had been making love to each other and the Hispanic guy ask me if I wanted to join in to which I answered no just give me the crack for making the run, so they gave me a bag and I went back into my brother William's bedroom and smoked it. Nevertheless, I had no rights, my brother William loved to berate me in front of his customers, both white and black, William would talk about how I had a college education, and here I was a dirty smelly junkie. I had two coats that I would wear in the winter time; one got burned by a fire in the trash can at the junk yard so it had a big hole in it. I would sleep in my three pairs of pants and three sweaters, under three blankets, and I could never seem to get warm in the winter time, I was always cold. I wore socks for gloves when I was outside and sometimes even when I was inside. And when it rained, at first you had to move the bed from one side of the room to the other side to stay dry, but as the months went on, the area of the ceiling that was not leaking became smaller and smaller, and soon, you just learned to live with getting wet. There was the bucket patrol, meaning you had to first place all these buckets under the leaks upstairs when it rained hard. Each bucket had a strategic preordained spot, to catch the optimum amount of water that was soon gushing from the roof which by now was leaking very badly. Which meant the ceiling in my room, the hallway the bathroom and the back bedroom? The back bedroom by this time had become uninhabitable due to water damage to the floor caused by the leaking roof; you could fall right through the floor. Then there was the task of emptying the buckets and trash barrels, which filled up faster than you would think, The buckets were never emptied to my brothers satisfaction, so there was always arguments about that, but if he felt good, and I was on time with the bucket emptying. I would get a hit of crack.

I was not allowed to keep food in my room, so I had to sneak food in, I lived for three years mostly on Murray's hotdogs, bread and sandwich cookies. I would take a single hot dog, uncooked of course, and split it into four pieces, the long way, them I would take four slices of bread, and make four raw hotdog sandwiches. I got used to eating a lot of raw food, my brother had a microwave oven but I was not allowed to use it, so I would buy frozen cooked fried chicken, and eat it after it thawed out. Soon I was getting donuts from Dunkin Donuts, They would throw out the donuts from the day before, they were perfectly good donuts to me they were just in the trash, and I would get a box of them out of the dumpster, and live off of them for a week. Soon the manager at the Dunkin Donuts saw me in the dumpster and locked the gate to keep me from getting the donuts, so I would climb over the gate, so the manger would put trash in with the donuts, old coffee grinds, dirt anything to make the donuts inedible, but I still got the donuts, just wiped them off. I would also stop at the pretzel factory and if I was lucky, I could get a few rows of soft pretzels out of their dumpster. But sometimes I was not smart enough to buy something to eat with my earnings and I would go hungry. I remember a few times after the drugs ran out, my stomach would be calling me to send down some food, so I would walk the few miles to Dunkin Donuts and the pretzel factory to raid their dumpsters. When I got there, weak from hunger and the walk, sometimes the dumpsters would be empty, I wanted too die, but I would walk back home and just be hungry. I would also accept handouts from people, they would give me their leftovers when they cleaned out their refrigerators, man, and I was a real bum.

I did all this became proficient in the junk metals game; I learned you had to get up early in the morning, about Five a.m., when the entire world was safe within their dreams, I walked the shadows. I learned at time I could rob people blind. You would be surprised how many people kept aluminum and copper in their backyard waiting to redeem it for cash, well people like me, we just cut out the middle man, them and took it to the junkyard for them. So for the next three years I jumped fences and got beat down if the people in the neighbored caught me, and I stole whatever I could get my hands on to support my drug habit. I stole children's bikes right from their yards, bags of aluminum cans, then I would meet Nick at the junkyard, and turn in my shit to get that wake-up hit, that it what crack addicts call the first hit of the day, a wake-up hit, you see Nick opened at 7 a.m. every day, and I would be copping drugs and in the house by seven thirty in the morning getting high. I had to give my brother his ten dollars and the rest I would smoke. By mid- morning I was done, so I had to go back out and get more money, this was particularly hard during the summer time when kids were out of school, the children would see me in all of my shame as I would be pushing my shopping cart. Now I had to hit the areas where there was trash being removed because it was to late in the day to climb into peoples yards, one thing about Latino areas is that they loved their beer, you could always get twenty or thirty dollars of beer cans from their trash on trash day. Of course you just had to dig in their trash bags at your own risk, and you never know what you would touch in those trash bags. There would be shitty diapers, rotted food, used cat litter, you got used to it, getting the cans to redeem them for cash was all that counted. Taking aluminum chairs from people's porches was of particular interest, their ladders from their yards. Once I got shot at through a back window by the owner of the house whose yard I was robbing, he missed of course, but that didn't stop me from robbing everything I could. I remember there were some great paydays. I remember I got up on my birthday, November 28th, got my shopping cart left at four in the morning, and did not return until two in the afternoon, it was the biggest load I ever had, I made almost a hundred dollars, and I smoked like a king all day.

The risk of being of beaten up was something you lived with and accepted. Once these three Hispanic males approached me and for no reason punched in the mouth about three in the morning. I ran of course and later came back to retrieve my shopping cart, my valuable shopping cart, my friend. Besides, it was full of aluminum, they had no idea how valuable what was in that shopping cart was to me. I would always hide my shopping cart because many other addicts would steal your shopping cart if they could they were very valuable. If I came out of my brothers house and my cart was missing, I would waste valuable time trying to steal someone else cart, and waste the whole morning and lose valuable stealing time trying to find another shopping cart. There was also the risk from your own black people, especially the young, black males. They looked at you as if you were a sub-human, you could be walking with your shopping car, and they would just attack you. Once I was just outside of Nicks, and these three black teens, attacked me out of know where, hit be in the head with a broom stick. I ran because the crack cocaine makes cowards of us all, and I had to wait for them to leave so I could go back to reclaim my precious cargo, my aluminum. I had to my aluminum to Nick's and redeem it and go get high. That was not the first time I got attacked, I came so close to death so many times, I was stealing other people's property.

Once I was stealing this radiator from a car I thought was abandoned but it was not, and the guy came running out the house and he hit me in the ribs with my own crowbar, then he shattered an aluminum window with glass in it over my head. I suffered three cracked ribs, but still I carried on, I had to support my habit. I went back home after the incident and smoked up the little money that I had, and after the crack wore off, I went into shock and I had to walk to the hospital. The emergency room at Temple University Hospital, and as I waited to be seen, these other young black guys were laughing at me because I was so skinny, I weighed about one hundred and fifty pounds. The doctor told me that I had to rest so that my cracked ribs would heal hell I was out there the next day jumping fences and stealing again. I was out there in the rain, the snow, the heat, it did not matter, I was a soldier, or so I thought. I remember I was out with my shopping cart one Christmas day, and this Hispanic lady gave me ten dollars to buy some food with, I bought crack instead, my addiction was a disease that knew no holidays and took no time off, it was twenty four seven every stinking day. The grind I called it.

Once when my brother William was locked up I went to cop some drugs late one night for a friend of my brothers at 8th and Ontario Streets and these Hispanic guys held me up. I was sitting on the step waiting for my drugs when this young boy walks up and puts a gun to my temple. Now this is how sick I was, I am thinking that if they rob me, I will not get a hit of crack for coming home empty handed, so I am calculating in my mind the risk factor of pushing his hand away and running, hoping he would not shoot me, but I could tell from the look in his eyes that he would kill me, so I gave him the money. The funny thing about that incident was that I knew the black drug dealer that was on duty that night; he had been to my brother's house and got high with us. Nevertheless he was just going to stand by and let those young boys kill me, man; there was no loyalty out in the streets. I was also called on by my brother to sell things for people when people came to the house to get high and they ran out of money. You know jewelry, home furnishings, I could sell anything, and did but there was always the risk of getting killed for it, and when the money ran out, people would sell everything, their children's clothes and sneakers. I hacked with my bothers car and picked people up and took them to where they wanted to go, right at Broad and Erie Avenue. I was living life on the edge, one time while hacking this guy gets into my car and ask me to take him to Germantown which I do. He was drug dealer and he got out to drop of some money, he left about one thousand dollars in the car on the back seat, I should have pulled off, but I wanted to be honest, I waited for him to come out and returned the money to him. He did not even give me a tip, I really kicked myself for not taking the money and running, and especially after the twenty dollars that he gave I was gone. Another time I saw these guys rob this cigarette truck at Broad and Erie Avenues, they took cases of Newport's and made a clean getaway, by the time I thought about going over there, they driver had returned, and I missed another chance. I thought that I was having a good time, but I was not anymore, it no longer was fun to get high anymore. It seemed as if I was just doing it now out of habit, the bloom was definitely off of this rose which was my addiction.

But something was wrong. I began to have nightmares about my daughter; I could not enjoy a high without thinking that my sister Vicky was at the front door, that my baby was involved in a terrible accident. It was the guilt preying on me, telling me that this was not right. Vicky bought Sandra over to see me one day, she did not even know who I was, she was so little, I held her, but part of me could not wait for them to leave, and part of me missed her when they did leave. I lived not to far from my mothers' house and many the times I went over her house to get tokens to go to a rehabilitation facility that did not exist Taking advantage of a mothers love; I would sell the tokens for drug money. I kept assuring her I had enough of getting high, but I used her hard earned money to get high. She would give me food when I was hungry, I was a mess. Nevertheless something was happening, I could no longer justify what I was doing, it became harder and harder, to justify my self degradation, and that is what kept me sick for so long, I could always justify my addiction to myself. I told myself that I had lived a good life, and if I died like this so be it; I had resigned myself to dying an addict. But God and fate had other plans for me, as I was about to find out

ACT THREE.
The Flight of the Phoenix

13

My Resurrection.

Like I said something was happening, but I had no idea what it was. I had endured so much pain for the last three years, that it was no longer fun to get high. It became like a full time job. Every waking moment of my life was spent in chasing that cloud in the pipe, sucking on that glass dick; I was stealing peoples aluminum doors, whatever, breaking into peoples property and stealing their copper plumbing. I was off the hook, but something was different, I wanted to stop, but could not stop. I had had enough of getting high in spirit, but not in mind, so I continued and the pain increased, the guilt increased, the nightmare on 10th street continued. I began to pray every day to God, I would beg, God, please stop or let me die because I cannot do this any more, but I kept on pushing that shopping cart as tears would be streaming down my face, and I also began to feel very embarrassed by the predicament that I was in. As friends I grew up with became aware of my condition, I was like a sideshow, someone to pity and yet feel good about because I had fallen so far from shinning so bright. And that's how some friends are, they want the best for you, but when you fall, you become the object of their scorn, and pity, someone to laugh at so that they do not feel so bad about themselves. Once I ran into Sedrick, a friend who I grew up with, he was driving his police car, and he offered me money. More than anything I wanted to take the money but I could not, I was so embarrassed that he saw me like that. I served in this capacity for a long time to quite a few people, to quite a few of my "friends'. And I prayed like this for one year, and when God decided that I had enough,

He began to move things for me. He stretched out his mighty hand, and caught me just like that. And it was over just like that.

I remember the day so clear, like it was yesterday; the day was November 19th, 1998, the day of my rebirth. It started like any other day, cold and wet, I had gotten up to get my shopping cart, it was 4 a.m. in the morning, and I proceeded to go into alleys and look over fences for things to steal which caused the dogs in the backyards to bark. I hated dogs because they always gave you away, the dogs would bark and alert people that you were in the alley. But wait I had some luck. This Hispanic guy had some aluminum rims in his yard, along with some car radiators made of copper. So I hopped his fence and began to steal his possessions. The rims had the tires on them, so it made it hard to get them over the fence. At this point things began to happen fast. He looked out his window and he spotted me, and yelled at me to get out of his backyard. He then pulled out his gun and shot twice at me. I only had enough time to get one tire because it was becoming daylight. I ran to my shopping cart, and raced for Nicks, now this guy calls the police, and as I am running down Old York Road, the police are rushing right past me. The guy is following me down the street and is talking to the police on his cell phone, he leads them to me. The police turn their cars around and rush to me with sirens wailing. The guy catches up to us, he identifies his belongings, punches me in the face. The police restrain him, and take me to jail. Just like that it is over, but I do not recognize that it is over for me yet. The police officers who arrested me told me I should have just left the shopping cart, but I could not because I was almost to the junk yard. I remember the load I had in my shopping cart, an aluminum ladder I had stole and some copper, whoever found my shopping cart after I was arrested came up.

So the police took me to Front and Westmoreland Streets to the police district. I kept asking the female police officer that arrested me, are you going to release me soon? And she kept answering that yes it would probably just be a fine. Little did I know that I would not see the light of day or the streets for 4 months? Now remind you it was about 7 a.m. in the morning when I arrived at the police station, so in my sick mind my addiction is playing head games with me, charting the course of time, how if I get out up to a certain point, how I can still make the junk yard which closes at three in the afternoon. As the hours slowly slipped away, I began to have to face the hard cold reality that I might not get high today, damn. So I began planning for tomorrow. And as I lay on the floor of the cell, I had to lay on the floor, because there was only one bed, and someone bigger than me had got there first, they had four of us stuffed into one cell meant to hold one person. So the other three of us slept on the floor, now came the hard part, probably the hardest part of my recovery. I had to deal with myself by myself, you see the drugs had always given me something to hide behind, now without the crack, my mind began to think a little clearer, remember I had a $100.00 a day habit for 12 years, can you imagine how much money I smoked up in that time? On the other hand, do not tell me.

So there I was lying on the ground in a police cell with three strangers, two of them who were just like me, drug users who got arrested for stealing as they were trying to support their drug habits, and one guy who was in for murder. I began to smell something funny at this time, it smelled like funky feet, I thought to myself. This guy lying next to me stinks I thought to myself, I could not escape that smell, and the odor was overwhelming me. Didn't anyone else smell this guy I thought? Then to my horror and surprise I realized what I smelled was myself, I smelled my own feet, and they must have been stinking like this for the last three years at least. Then I was overcome by what I was, I was smelly, dirty and disgusting, it was me, this is what I had become. I began to weep to my self inside myself, which it had come to this. After twelve hours in the police station I was informed that I was going down to the Roundhouse, again, I would not be released, so I waited for the police van to take all four of us to the Roundhouse. By that time, it was evening, and I had not had anything to eat all day, now there have been days where I had not eaten, but the crack took care of that, so without the crack, I began to get very hungry. They finally gave us the standard cheese sandwich and eight ounces of juice, just enough to keep you alive .Then we arrived at the Roundhouse. You know this how sick I was I was still trying to calculate how long it would take me to get home if I was released from the Roundhouse, I still had that metal grate stashed you know, but I even then did not realize that the gig was up.

They placed me into a holding cell because I could not be in general population, or the Bubble it was called, I had too many outstanding warrants against me, so I knew I was going up to State Road, to the county prisons. I was at the roundhouse two days, getting fed once very twelve hours, but I had the fortunate luck of getting a heroin addict for a cell mate. He was sick from going cold turkey, they did not really care if you have a habit in jail, there are no methadone programs or medication, no detox, and you just have to suffer. So while he was so sick, he gave me all his food to eat. That was the trade off, he gave me his food and I took care of him. Without being high, it was as if I had not eaten in three years. My body craved food, and he gave me his sandwiches, and so I took care of him, but it was terrible to watch somebody go cold turkey from a heroin addiction. There was talk that we would be shipped to the prison and a regular criminal told me it would be much better, we would eat better because we would get a cold pack. A cold pack, what the hell was that, I thought. Well, I was about to find out what a cold pack was.

So we were transferred by bus up to the new prison called C.F.C.F, it was a state of the art facility, named for some former orison board director or something. As soon as we got there, we received our first cold pack. It was a lunch pack that came with two sandwiches, a juice, a little Debby snake cake and a piece of fruit, I was in heaven, so after I ate, we had to be processed, we were placed in a holding cell, and I had a chance once again to take stock of myself. I was dirty, malnourished and I smelled. I remember I tried to get rid of the smell from my sock, they had little sinks in the cells, and I kept washing my socks over and over and they would not come clean. I kept washing them, the water kept getting dirty. I began to understand how dirty I was. So we began to get processed and they moved us along like we were on a conveyer line from one processing point to another. I was so dirty that the guards would not even touch my clothes; they had to put on gloves to pick the clothes up with and to dispose of them. They pointed me toward the showers, and it felt so good when I got in the shower. It was the first shower for me in years and I was beginning to feel like a human being again. The guards gave us another cold pack to eat, then I saw a familiar face, it was my neighborhood friend Charles Green, he was a prison guard that I grew up with. When I first came back to Philadelphia, before the drugs ruined my life, Charles and another childhood friend of mines would run various activities for the neighborhood we grew up in, you know to give something back to the neighborhood. We ran basketball programs in the summer time, and a festival to commemorate our area, we worked very closely together, and I had not seen him for many years. It hurt both of us for me to be in this situation, but at least his was a friendly face. He looked out for me as best he could, with extra food and what have you and that meant a lot to me because I was so hungry When we got to the processing area where the guards wanted you to fill out a phone list so that you could call your family or to receive phones call, I was so embarrassed that I could not remember any of my family member's phone numbers. And that was tragic, because unknown to me, my family who were on the outside were having a fit. By the third day that I was missing, my brother had alerted my family that I was missing. My family then went about the chore of trying to find me. They thought I was dead; they began searching hospitals, the morgue, missing person reports. What I did to my mother and family I can never forgive myself for and this is something for all addicts to think about, the total pain we cause our families. Because the misery that we put ourselves through as addicts, our families go experience it also. The pain the suffering that we feel we project all of that on to them, and for a mother to look for her child, thinking he is dead, that is a burden I live with every day. The burden keeps me strong and from going back out there to use drugs again, that and my God. So my sister Sharon calls my cousin Beverly who is a parole officer and asks that she run my name to see if I had been arrested, my name came up on Beverly's computer, and so there was a sense of relief from my family.

They gave me an orange jumpsuit to wear at the prison, and a pair of sneakers that were two sizes too small. I slept on the floor until they had bed space for us in the prison. C.FC.F. was a state of the art prison, one of those prisons for profit deals, so everything was done differently. Rehabilitation was carried out with an eye on the bottom line, profit. So everything was geared toward turning a profit, at the expense of the inmates of course. The meals were horrendous. The meals were computer calculated so that each man received the minimum daily requirements just above starvation; it was just enough food to keep you alive. Like little snacks that they serve in daycare to small children that is how big the micro-wave meals were. They controlled you with a little amount of food, so if you were too weak to cause a problem that is what they wanted. I was in the cell with a cool guy; he was in for non-payments of his child support. Nevertheless every meal was an experience in hunger, because you were just as hungry after the meal as you were before you ate, but I got used to the daily routine, and accepted my fate. I signed some papers for my transfer to another prison, and on Thanksgiving morning at about 5 a.m., the guards woke us up, and we were being moved to the "Creek" or the house of corrections as it was called, it was an old 19th century jail. So I spent Thanksgiving Day 1998, in a holding cell with about 30 other prisoners, waiting for the next shift of guards to check us in. We watched as the guards ate their Thanksgiving meal, and the guards watched the Dallas Cowboys on television, while we ate another cold pack. I was still grateful; I was eating better than I had in years, but I vowed that I would not spend another holiday in prison because while we were all stuffed in this holding cell, a profound thing happened to me. There was a guy, about sixty five years old, an older addict, a tired addict, a worn out addict, he was incarcerated for some minor offense, but all he talked about was getting out and getting his social security check and getting high again and going tricking. This was all he had to look forward too, when most men his age are retired or thinking about retirement, he was still working at the hardest job on earth, being an addict. I said to myself right then and there, if you do not change your life, this will be you in twenty five years, I could not go out like that, and I had to change. I was determined to change; this older man had given me another wake up call, one of many I received in jail.

So I was transferred that evening, to a cell block in the Creek and it seemed like it was a mile long. There were two televisions at each end of the block as it was called and it had about 100 guys cramped into this little space. There were two prison guards on duty for all of these men. Nevertheless the prisoners had a pecking order, a block captain, a co-captain like it was a community. And it was a community we just could not leave or go anywhere. This is what it jail was all about, either you were there for selling drugs or using drugs. I was taken back to the police district for my hearing, and my sister Sharon was there, I did not even recognize her, but she was there, Sharon later told me what I had on and everything. I was taken back to jail, because I had four bench warrants, which means I did not show up for court appearances too many times before. So I was being held in jail with no chance for bail, and that was good, because it was taken out of my hands by God, and put in his hands. So I began to sober up for the first time in 10 years. I began to eat on a regular basis, they gave me a JVC haircut, you are entitled to one free one, and there was so much hair on my head that you could have stuffed a pillow with it. Nevertheless life in prison was no piece of cake; there was a lot of adjusting on my part. One particular day, the other inmates were about to kill this inmate because they thought he had stole a pair of socks from another inmate. The prison guards quietly exited the cell block, and about a hundred guys worked themselves up into frenzy. The cell block captain named Brice led the way shouting that if you steal from one of us you steal from all of us, and just as they were about to massacre this guy, they found the inmates missing socks. So the inmates and Brice the block captain began to get worked up against the accuser if you falsely accuse on of us you falsely accuse all of us they shouted, and they let the falsely accused inmate beat the shit out the accuser, it was a surreal atmosphere. I was in a cell with a young guy. You know the young black men of our generation are in jail for procession to distribute drugs. That is what all the young guys were there for, intent to deliver drugs. This was the fate of our young black men, to be held on charges of possession with the intent to deliver drugs. Somehow the American Dream had changed into the American nightmare. The American Dream went from getting an education and getting to married and raising the nuclear family, to being jailed for possession with intent to deliver drugs; somehow these young black men got all mixed up. Nevertheless the older inmates were there for committing crimes to support the drug trade and to buy drugs, you know like petty theft and shoplifting. The older addicts like me were there to support the young guys who were there for possession of drugs with intent to deliver, who do you think that they were going to deliver the drugs too? They were going to deliver the drugs to guys like me.

Nevertheless, I began to shower everyday, and to put on clean clothes, I had my county blues that they gave me which is just a pair of blue khakis and a blue shirt. Nevertheless I began to feel like I wanted to change, and I began to pray every night which is something that I had not done in a long time. I began to talk about rehabilitation to other drug addicts like me; there was this one guy in particular. We had started this journey together, from the Front & Westmoreland police district, to the Roundhouse and to the Creek. So we hung together, because we had a common bound. We both confessed that we wanted to change. We talked every day about getting out and changing our lives. They told me my court appearance would not be until February of 1999, so I settled in with the daily routine. I spent my birthday November 28th and Christmas in jail, then they called my name shortly after Christmas, and I learned that I was going to be discharged. The jails were overcrowded; there was a court order from the state that capped off the prison population at a certain level, and those inmates without any drama were being released. No drama meant you did not commit a felony or violent crime. I got so scared because I was not ready to leave jail yet, but I had to. I really wanted to stay in jail, being incarcerated had become my safe haven, I sort of liked being locked up. I really wanted to go to a rehabilitation facility and the social worker in jail promised me that I would when I went to court in February

They processed me and three other guys; one was my friend who I talked so much to about recovery. The guards at the prison gave us some old clothes to wear, and with these shoes two sizes to small, I was sent back into the world. The three of us walked to Bridge and Pratt to catch the subway, and I was scared. I didn't know what to do. I got on the Broad street line after transferring of the Market- Frankford elevated subway line, as the train rocketed down the tracks, I asked God to show me the way, do I go past the stop that leads me to my mother and sisters on Broad and Dauphin Streets, or do I continue onward to the stop where my brother William lived, and continue on the path of my self destruction. My friend got off at his stop, and declared that he was going to get him hit of crack, that I didn't go with him was my first test. I later learned that he had died from a drug overdose, which very easily could have been me; I then realized how difficult it would be to stay clean. This is no lie, as I approached the stop to my mother and sisters' house, something picked me up by the collar, and escorted me off the train, the choice was made, and God intervened again. In spite of myself, I would choose life over death.

14

A Family Reunion.

My family was so happy to see me when I arrived at my sisters' house, it was like I had returned from a war or something, and you know I guess that I did. Because the war on drugs is a real conflict that takes peoples lives everyday, except I was no longer causality, I was no longer missing in action. That song from the Ojay's seemed so appropriate, a Family Reunion that song played in my head as I was re-introduced to my family. It felt so good to be clean, and I wanted to continue this precious gift from God. So I saw my daughter Sandra for the first time in over a year, she was almost three years old now. I stayed at the same house where so much of my misery had taken place, the house on 28th street, my Mom-mom's house. My brother Douglas was still getting high in the back room; I wanted no part of that. My mother gave me ten dollars and the first time in years I did not spend the money she gave me for drugs. My sister Robin worked for Horizon House, a reha-bilitation facility, she got me the contact numbers to call, B.S.H.I., and they got me in touch with Self Help Inc. I was to go in on Monday, it was Friday, and I was forty three years old, and I was scared to death. I spent the weekend with my daughter, to remind me what I was fight-ing for. I even smoked some weed, the last time I used anything to get high with, I geuss I needed it for courage, and on Monday morning, I boarded the bus, for the long ride to Self Help Inc. I had put off going to Self Help Inc. at first, they were ready to take me on Friday, but I put it off until Monday, and when that day came I could delay it no longer. I had to catch two subways and a bus, I thought I was going to the end of the world, and I was scared, for the first time in a long time,

I was scared. I wondered if anyone on the bus knew I was a drug addict. It seemed as if everyone on the bus was staring at me. No was staring at me of course, they were to busy living life on life's terms, going to work and all, looking back on the situation no one even noticed me. Nevertheless, I still asked myself; did they notice the green trash bag that served as my luggage? It seemed that they were watching me; I looked so out of place. Nevertheless it had been a long time since I rode a bus sober. I took in the sights and sounds of normalcy, people going to work, children going to school. The world as I had known it before drug addiction really did still exist, there were still normal people doing normal things. I had been around addicts for so long that I had forgotten that this normal world still existed. I took in the sight and sounds of this normal world that I had not been a part of for so long, it felt strange but good, and I was back in the real world for the first time in ten years. I got to the Bridge and Pratt subway elevated train stop and waited to catch the bus to Self Help Inc., I clutched my directions that I had written on a piece of paper, looked at them over and over to make sure I was catching the right bus. So I began this ride, a ride that would forever change me and the direction of my life, and lead me to recapture my spirituality and who I was.

I had just a plastic bag with a few clothes my mother had given me, and I arrived at Self Help and I was scared. I was greeted by Carmelo Benjamin, the intake supervisor he talked to me and began to process me, afterward he asked if I was hungry, I said yes and I was taken down to the kitchen to get something to eat, I was reassured by one of the clients Kevin who worked in the kitchen. As he served me my food he told me that everything would be alright, and you know what, I believed him. So they completed my intake, and I quickly realized how lucky I was. It was an all male facility, they gave each person his own bedroom, and it was a nine month inpatient program, it was perfect for me. God had looked out for me again. So I settled in, and was not afraid anymore. I moved to the first phase unit which is where the new clients are housed so that they can adjust to the facility and the program, and quickly made friends with the new guys as we were called. I had my own room, privacy to an extent, and was able to shower each day, to eat a healthy meal; I ate everything I could get my hands on. The guys who were there from jail made fun of me, they called me twenty two slim because of my slender waist, and because I weighed one hundred and forty pounds when I arrived at Self Help Inc. Nevertheless I quickly found out what Self Help Inc. was. It had guys off the street like me, and guy's court stipulated to complete the program, and if the court stipulated guys left the program they would be arrested and sent back to jail. That arrangement also meant that some were there for help and some because they had to be there, I was there for help. Self Help Inc. meant just what it said, you either helped yourself, or you were doomed to repeat the same mistakes that landed you there in the first place It was set up with about eighty-five guys, and I will never forget the first speech that one of the counselors that worked at Self Help Inc. Mr. Robert Bullock gave to the assembled group the first time we had group. He said that ninety five percent of us would fail, that ninety-five percent of the guys in the room were going to go back to jail, or they were going to use drugs again or that they were going to die. I looked around the room and thought to myself he was crazy, all of us could make it. But you see he had thirteen years experience doing this, and he was right. I looked around the room and decided that I would be one of the five percent that made it. I humbled myself, and accepted anything they told me to do; nothing was too much to do if it meant that I would get better, it was a lot better than I had lived for the last ten years. The guys from prison, most of whom were there for selling drugs looked on us addicts, their former customers with disdain, they laughed at me. I was so skinny that I ate double portions at every meal; I just could not seem to get full. It seemed like I had not eaten in years and I was trying to make up for it. My friend Mr. T. and I, we ate everything that was not nailed down, breakfast, lunch and dinner. I knew Mr. T. from the neighborhood around 15th and Poplar streets, he had a hit house like mines down near the Richard Allen projects located at 12th and Parrish Streets, and he was sent to Self Help Inc. from jail. We worked in the kitchen for months and he was a big part of my recovery, we would go to the gym at Self Help Inc. after we had dinner when we were allowed to use it and lift weights, I learned to work on the outside as well as the inside.

They had strict rules, they woke you up at six a.m. for breakfast, and after breakfast then we cleaned the kitchen. Then those who took it went upstairs for medication, and then you were given permission to go back to your room and clean up and prepare for the day. Clean up meant that you had to clean the whole area where your room was located, and then you had to wait for inspection, after inspection you then went to group therapy all day long. We broke for lunch, and then you had your afternoon general group therapy. You were then allowed to go back to your room for a few minutes before dinner, and then you cleaned up after dinner, and were allowed to go back to your room for showers. After showers we got to go to the gym, or relax or whatever, then at ten you cleaned the main hall and went to bed. You could not be on the phases without a spot, that meant someone had to accompany you where ever you went, you could not go to the bathroom without permission, They rules coming out of our asses, but you know what I needed that structure because without it I would have not recovered. I loved to be there, and for the first six weeks you were on blackout which meant that you could not have contact with anyone form the outside world; you only had access to the phone on Thursday and Saturday, and only for ten minutes after your blackout was over. We cleaned and cleaned and cleaned again, you would be called out of bed in the middle of the night to clean the main hall. I volunteered for kitchen duty the last six months of my stay; I was also the librarian for Self Help Inc. which I really enjoyed.

It seemed like I was going to court every week for the open cases I had when I first got to Self Help Inc., but God took care of all that. In one case the District Attorney who was prosecuting tried to talk me into taking a plea bargain with one thousand hours of community service, we both knew that the store that I was charged with shoplifting from was out of business, Clover was the store, and so I beat the rap. I had to go before Federal court for the check stealing and while I waited for the trial I court stipulated to remain in the program so now I was just like the guys from the county court system. The trail was so scary because I did not know if they were going to lock me up, but the judge and prosecutor were so impressed at how I had changed my life that I was given probation, and placed with a federal parole officer, he was a good guy. I had to take weekly urine test to prove that I was sober, but it was alright, I was clean and had nothing to hide. One by one the cases were handled by my higher power and the courts, and after that last case was adjudicated I could focus on my recovery, and begin to understand why I was here. But life at Self Help Inc. was no fun either, we had a counselor, our therapist who was supposed to run our group therapy, well he relapsed after thirteen years clean, his name was Al Ferrante. I really loved Al, but after his relapse, there was no way he could be our therapist. So for the first three months of treatment, we got no treatment, as they tried to figure out what to do with us. Finally we got an untrained therapist to lead our group. But I did most of my own treatment. I was not to be deterred, and Al Ferrante's relapse kept it real for me. As did the relapse of my best friend Mr. T, he relapsed on the first home weekend pass we went on, so they took his weekend passes for the next four months, almost until he graduated. Then upon graduation from the program, he relapsed again. Guys were relapsing left and right at Self Help Inc., you would think that being in a drug rehabilitation facility they would understand why they were there, but they did not. I saw many friends relapse, I was determined that it would not be me. They offered G.E.D. classes to the clients at the facility, but most of the clients that did not graduate high school played in class and did not learn a thing. It seemed that many of the clients were incapable of change, but like one of the counselors said, I could measure my progress against their failure. So they served a purpose, one of the ones who failed was a white friend of mines who lived next door to me, we played chess a lot. His mother was so proud of him for turning his life around, he was court stipulated to be there and to finish the nine month program. I can never say that I saw death in his face, but he was destined to die. He died on New Years Eve right after graduating the program. He died of a heroin overdose, apparently his body was not accustomed to amount that he shot up with after not doing drugs for so long and it killed him. I felt so bad for his mom, who came to see him every weekend, can you imagine what that holiday will do to her for the rest of her life? She came up to spend the holidays with us out of a need to reflect because she had no where else to go. There was a fellow client who I thought was my friend, he used me to get to another program by accusing me of committing a homosexual advance toward him, which of course was a lie. They transferred him thanks to Nick my counselor friend, and I learned again how deep this illness runs in us. He had used me because he wanted to get transferred to the Veterans Administration Hospital; he was not the first and certainly would not the last person to use a friend As Mr. Bullock's prediction began to unfold, many more clients died or went back to jail.

Many of the guys from jail were not there for recovery so they made it very hard for those of us who were. They would disrupt the house and cause all kinds of mayhem when they could, especially at the weekly Narcotics Anonymous meetings. We had three mandatory weekly meetings that we had to attend that were in house, and this was my first exposure to Narcotics Anonymous. You got to hear stories not unlike your own from other addicts as they shared and then you got to share yourself, it was very therapeutic to learn that there was recovery going on out in the world. Then you would hear stories from the court stipulated clients, they would relate more bullshit than a little bit, their job was to slow down the meetings with their antics and jokes, they definitely were not there for recovery. But even they served a purpose, they were their for you to judge how well your recovery was going, through them you could see just how far you had come, if you no longer got involved with their bullshit, then you as a person were making progress. If you could see through their crap, if you no longer attempted to make sense out of non-sense, then that meant that you were getting better, or at least that's how it was explained to me by a friend of mine.

15

Spiritual Recovery:

If there is one thing I learned at Self Help Inc. it was about the spiritual recovery of me. Recovering from drugs I had to recover myself from myself, which is the hardest thing that I have ever had to do, that may sound a little confusing but I will attempt to explain it. I was my own worst enemy during my addiction as any addict is, there is nothing as bad as an educated addict, and I believed that I could stop at anytime, due to my superior intellect. I was very mistaken, and that mistaken belief kept me sick for a lot longer than necessary, I found out that I needed much more than intellect to defeat my disease; I needed God and my spiritual strength. Through God, I was able to surmise what I need to do to arrest my disease, and help my recovery by addressing my recovery like a triad. This means I had to deal with myself on three levels, the spiritual level, the mental level and the physical level. Why I had not been able to recover before was because I only dealt with my addiction as a mental or physical problem, and I was ill equipped to handle this beast that controlled me. It is because it was an attack proper on my soul, and I never dealt with it on that level, was never enlightened on that level, and never knew the truth about the strength that I processed on the spiritual level. Conventional therapy reshapes and deals with the physical person, medical treatment to address the ravages of the disease on the body through medication and medical care, then you were subjected to mental therapy that is supposed to help you deal with the psycho-social ramifications of your actions and your addiction, and what we did as men and women to acquire the drug. Nevertheless, the most important part of any recovery is the rebirth of my God given right to my spirituality; it is the one thing that connects us to our higher power. It gives us our power and strength as a speceis, and also gives us the moral strength, the physical strength and the spiritual strength to resist the evils of the world and change our lives. I am not talking about a religion, or any practiced rituals of a par-ticular religion, I am talking about spiritual strength which comes from God and that we can harness irregardless of the religion that we believe in. I was lucky enough to acquire this spiritual strength through two sources. The ladies that came at minister to us where non-demonical, they just believed in God. They were all in their seventies and eight-ies, but I admired their dedication and their spiritual strength. They would come to minister to us, faithfully, rain or shine, snow or sleet, every Wednesday, it was like clockwork. We would sing spiritual songs, read scripture and fellowship, those ladies were the best. Then we had a black male pastor who would come on Thursday nights to minister too us, he taught me so much about the real me. The one who I been running from all my life, to face who I am, and to make a difference, I was born to be a leader of our people, I have the gift of communica-tion, but I ran from who I was, sought refuse in drugs and alcohol, but God would not let me slide, he would not let me die, and now" I BEGAN TO REALIZE WHY". I had a job to do, and I could no longer run from it, my destiny had arrived. The bible study and men's spiritual class were very important. Like I said, I needed that spiritual strength to get my life back on track. I began to attend church services and regained my spirit and physical strength. Most of the other clients made fun of our church services, but it helped a lot, I remember an addict named Benny that would come to services with us every time that we had them he had Aids, and relapsed after completing the pro-gram at Self Help Inc. he left his clothes and everything. Benny would talk about how dirty he was, just like I was and he would talk about how these drug dealers beat him so bad for stealing some drugs from them that Benny shit on himself, I was sure that he would make it for his kids, but it was not meant to be.

My fifth month into the program I earned the right to go home on weekend passes, I would leave Saturday morning, and I had to return

Sunday by six in the evening. I loved it, it gave me a chance to spend time with my family, especially my daughter Sandra, she was almost four years old now, and my sister Vicky was waiting for me to finish the program so that I could take responsibility for her. We would spend weekends together at my sister Robin's house, and I would take her to see her mother Sandi, who seemed uninterested. She was in recovery by now, but her recovery was not going as smoothly as mine. I had to have an operation because the doctor found a tumor in my chest, I went into the hospital and they took it out. I was so afraid that I was going to die after coming this far in my recovery. Nevertheless my mother who is very spiritual said not to worry, God had it under control and he did. The operation was a success and a mass the size of my fist was removed from my chest. They put a tube in there to drain the blood; I went back to Self Help Inc. and was placed on bed rest. The next morning my sheets in my bed were covered with blood. They rushed me to the hospital where the doctor reopened the wound and inserted another tube for draining, I had to change the dressing twice a day. But I was even okay with that, nothing could faze me now, I was growing stronger in my recovery everyday.

It was at this time that everything was revealed to me. I was lying in my room, feeling very depressed after my operation, trying to deal with where my life had taken me, weak from the loss of blood and angry that no one in my family had come to see me after my operation. At this point, God determined that I was ready to hear his voice. I heard him speak to me. He told me that I was saved for a reason, and then he told me what the reason was. To spread the message about spiritual recovery, and then I began to write down what had happened to me the last nine months, through this, he told me to name this program The Millennium Foundation Inc., and that this program would help many people in the future. God told me what the program should include, and how to save hundreds of oppressed people. He told me he would take care of everything, so I wrote it all down. Then I felt this great sense of peace, finally I was at peace with myself. I felt this great sense of joy and spiritual harmony, I at last knew now why I was here. I still have the original writings from that day, I cherish them as a message from above, and so I knew what I had to do with my life. God had saved my life, and he wanted something in return, I would repay this debt.

I went to my sister's wedding that weekend, against the doctors' advice, but I was not going to miss it for the world. It was the first function that I could attend since I entered Self Help Inc, and my family wanted me there, so I went and almost bled to death, and I missed my check in time at six p.m. You are supposed to check in by six p.m. Saturday evening on your weekend pass to let the supervisor at Self Help Inc. know that you are alright, and I missed it. So I lost my next weekend, which gave me more time to rest and refine the program that The Millennium Foundation Inc, would become. I graduated the next week, and moved upstairs with the graduates, we had more freedom than the regular clients, paid rent, got a key to my room and I got a job. There were restrictions on us graduates, we had to attend a weekly graduate meeting that was held at Self Help Inc. and we had to be in the building by eleven at night, unless we had an overnight job. I was able to see my daughter whenever I wanted, but it was time to take responsibility for her. My sister Victoria, God bless her soul had raised my daughter with Robin as their own, but it was time for me to step up and be a man., and a father. I stayed at Self Help Inc. for nine more months, and in April of 2000, I got an apartment, and took custody of my daughter. I later went to court and got full custody, my daughter's mother did not show up for the hearing, I never knew why.

Giving Back To Those less Fortunate.

I took a year long commitment at the Parkview Hospital detox to run the Saturday meeting for Narcotics Anonymous through Hospitals and Institutions or H. & I. It was important for me to give something back to the addicts that were still out there suffering in their addictions, just as it had been given to me, and to see the pain of their faces fresh from their self destructive binges. I gave them my hope and strength and they gave me their pain, which kept it real for me. It was so important to me to do it that I would be late picking up my daughter on my weekend visits but it was worth it because good deeds for others is the rent we pay for our time here on earth. So I did this every Saturday until they closed down the facility, I got some good speakers to come and share their hope, many were counselors at Self Help Inc and had helped me through my trials and tribulations over the nine months that I was there like the late Billy Kerns, Nate Williams, and Rick, they were strong meetings, giving something to those who listened, to me and those who shared. I saw so much pain at Parkview Hospital and that pain helped me to steel my resolve to not fail in my recovery. I would see people who were really beat up from the drugs; they were still very fresh in their pain, the look of their addictions still fresh on their faces. I worked with Robert Bullock whom I knew from Self Help Inc. and we would run great meetings, it really helped me to stay clean. I saw people from all walks of life, former nurses, parents, sons and daughters, all kinds of people that kept it real for me; I was determined to never sit on the other side of the table again. I also would go up to Self Help Inc. every year on my anniversary and share my story for Andrew, he ran the meetings at Self Help Inc, for years, including when I was a client there. Andrew was a former heroin addict who had been clean for ten years, he had came through Self Help Inc. and came back to run the Sunday Narcotics Anonymous meeting so every around November the 19th, I would make that trip to Self Help Inc and share my story to the clients still there.

I was so afraid of this little person who was my daughter that I barely knew, but I know that she loved me to death and I loved her, and she was glad to have me back in her life. So we got an apartment, with her own room, she never had that living with my sister, but she ended up in my bed every night anyway. I remember when I went to see the apartment, at Lindley Towers, it was owned by a white man named Lockwood Smith, and he was British I think. So I go to see him and interview for the apartment, I had no references of course, but he was so impressed with my resolve that he gave me the apartment and when Sandy and I went to pick up our keys, he welcomed my daughter by saying, "Welcome home little lady", he always called my daughter little lady. So we moved in the next week and everyone helped out, my brother Alan, my sister Vicky, my mother and her friend Sonny and my late brother William. I had no furniture except the hand-me-downs that my mother gave me; one sofa was so roach infested me had to fumigate it before we took it in. Nevertheless, it did not matter, I was so happy to have a place of my own, after having lived at Self Help Inc, in the graduate program for nine months; I was finally free to live life on life's terms. My mother set up Sandy's bedroom, made the bed up after my brother Alan put it together, I set my bedroom up, and we waited for the used refrigerator to be delivered. I remember the first time that Sandy and I went food shopping. I remember the first time we went to Olney Plaza at front and Olney Avenue to go clothes shopping for school; I remember it like it was yesterday.

I learned about parental responsibility, taking her to school. Teachers conferences, and having her around 24/7, I got used to that, cooking dinner for us every night. I also got used to getting Sandra's hair done and just sharing my love with her. The one thing that I thank God for is that she was to young to remember me as a junkie, all of her memories are of the man she grew to know and love, I thank God for that everyday. I got a job working at Girard Medical Center, working with the mentally ill and drug addicts. I dove into my work and worked many long hours to make a better life for me and my child. I worked many 16 hour days, The Millenium Foundation Inc, got pushed to the back burner as I struggled to survive. Nevertheless working at Girard medical center was important for me; it gave me a chance to help others as I had been helped, to see that the sick and suffering still reside on our cities streets. To keep me focused on my recovery and give something back, which is what my job gave me, but the system that I worked within would not allow me to truly help the sick people that we were supposed to be helping. It seemed that we operated a revolving door that only helped the patients on a short term basis and then set the patients up for failure, so that they would return to the hospital and the system could continue to make money off of the patients. I quickly became disillusioned and cynical. Then in 2003, I had to leave work I was depressed and almost had a nervous breakdown from working almost eighty hours a week, also as a result of my long work load my daughter was suffering form lack of attention. It seemed as if we were never home to enjoy the new home I bought for us. So God slowed me down again, He reminded me of the pact we made. It was time to repay my debt to him.

The Reality of Death:

But there was also pain; one Saturday while I was at work I got a phone call from my sister, my sister Sharon called me and told me that my nephew James had been killed in a car crash the night before, he was just sixteen. James was the second of my brother William's sons to die at the age of sixteen, William Blake being the other, I can remember when Billy-boy as we called William Blake would spend the night over the house on 15th Street, I remember that he loved oodles of noodles, I remember how I begged God to watch over him, as I did with James, and I remember when I heard that he had died. I was still getting high when I found out that he was killed, we were at my brother's house smoking crack, and watching the 11:00 p.m. news, when they announced the he had been murdered. I also can remember that I was too high to go to the funeral, to high to say goodbye, I was and still am very ashamed about that, that I was too high to say goodbye to William Blake. As a matter of fact, I was robbing this abandoned house of an electric generator the day of the funeral. These were two young lives snuffed out by the streets, and drugs. James had left the boys home he had been placed in and started to live on the streets, selling drugs and fighting for drug dealers. His face was scared from his fights as he fought for acceptance in the streets. I cursed God; I had prayed to him every night and begged him for James safety. I felt betrayed and I felt that God had let me down by allowing James to die like that. I went into the storeroom on 2ADC in the hospital that I worked in and cried, they asked me if I wanted to leave work, I did not because I felt helpless and working helped me get through it. The funeral was at his grand-mother Emma's church, and as I looked at him lying in the coffin, I could not help but be overwhelmed with images of him as a little boy, riding his bike, eating oodles of noodles, and just being a little boy who never had a chance in life. My own failure to him preyed on my mind, and the part I had played in his fate could not be forgotten by me. I cry now even as I write this, on the inside and on the outside.

The toll that drugs have taken on my life and the lives of my family has been devastating and overwhelming, but it is no more devastating for us than for many families in Philadelphia both black and white. The pain and suffering we endure as we bury our young, our loved ones and our friends is overwhelming, yet we must continue to endure, to carry on in their memory so that their passing has not been in vain. We must continue to resist and turn this thing around before we are all consumed and kill each other out of ignorance and misunderstanding. If I can make one person understand this, then this book has not been in vain.

I burned myself out working at Girard Medical Center, a com-munity hospital run by incompetent managers, although the people I worked with on the ward were great, the hospital itself was ripe with incompetence, from Community Behavioral Health, to the people who ran the place. What the government does to the mentally ill is a true crime, overuse of pharmaceuticals and far to short hospital stays for the sick, and I worked with and say some strange things. Suicidal patients, and fake patients, drug addicts trying to beat the system, and things the average person would never believe, that I no longer work there is a blessing to me, but we must not forget the people who care for those in our society that most people do not care about. They are the true heroes, and I will never forget my experiences and growth with them, it was a true honor.

So I slowed down, began to enjoy life, and started The Millennium Foundation Inc. in late 2003. It took almost a year and a half for us to receive our 501(c) 3 nonprofit status, but I persevered. We ran our first program with the help of the Drexel University Alumni Association at Christmas time 2004. With a one hundred dollar donation from Citizens Bank, the foundation in conjunction with my sister's Victoria and Sharon's churches gave out 100 holiday baskets to low-income families. I felt so proud and good, I was doing what God required from me. I now have the courage to work for myself, and God, to purchase real estate, and take this foundation out into the world. We are attempting to build low-income housing in Philadelphia As I finish this book, and look to the future, I do so unafraid. For I stand here, a testament and a monument to the power of God in our lives. With the message for all that you can recover from anything in your life, weather it is drugs, crime whatever. With the reconnection to God through your spiritual self, all things are possible, all odds can be overcome. All things are attainable. God is great; God is good, all the time. I still struggle with my spirituality, I still struggle with doing the right thing, it is so easy to do the wrong things, sometimes I want to steal things just for no reason, sometimes I want to be bad like I was before, it is a daily battle with my inner demons, they do not go away, the are still with me, I just have learned to hold them at bay. Once you have crossed over to the dark side of yourself, and discovered just how evil you can be, the journey back is a life long journey I believe. I never want to hold a gun or shoot a gun again in my life, I never want to hurt another human being through the selling of drugs, but I struggle within my self every waking moment of every day with what I was, and what I am still capable of. Even now when I relate what had happened to me to co-workers, it seems as if the whole thing was an out of body experience, did it all really happen, or was I dreaming. Was all the pain and misery real? Or did I make it up, I sometimes cannot believe that these experiences were real, but they were, and I must not forget that least I repeat them.

As I finished my book and people read it, I found out that this book touched a lot of lives . There was the young lady who bought a copy, She was about to be wed to a man that was in recovery from drug addiction like myself, She expressed to me how reading Street Corner Symphony gave her a better understanding of what her fiance' was going through on a daily basis as he continued to recover from his illness. This lady even invited me to her wedding which I though was nice. There were many stories and experiences that readers shared with me about growing up in Philadelphia. I had no idea that my story would touch so many lives, but it did. I hoped that it would but still I had no idea that it would. As I sit here writing my final thoughts, it is Monday, September 25th and I am reminded about how much has changed and how much has not. You see a five year old child was shot to death on Sunday in Strawbeery Mansion. She was shot along with her grandmother and another child as they were caught in the crossfire between two groups of young black males trying to kill each other. The gun violence in Philadelphia has become unimaginable, as the memorials rise up on street corners throughout the city, street corners filled with teddy bears and candles, they become a grim reminder to our apathy and to our surrender to the tugs that would destroy us. They become a reminder to another young life snuffed out far to soon, before she even had a taste of life. She could have been the mayor when she grew up, she could have cured a disease, or even cured cancer, but we will never know now, because she is dead.

About this time I began to work for Compro-Tax North Philly. I had met Tim the manager one day while I was looking for information for my non-profit organization. I took a tax class and was exposed to a new beginning; I met black people who were not afraid to be entrepreneurs like Jim, also Wilson and Sharon. I also met Mr. Jackie Mayfield. I met Janise and Agee; I was introduced to the Matah Network and the teaching of the late Ken Bridges. I lost my job at North Philadelphia Health Systems, and never looked back. Although I cherished my job at Girard Medical Center, God told me it was time to leave, time to strike out on my own, time to work for my own dreams as apposed to someone else dreams, time to repay my debt to God.

The Terrible Toll of Drugs:

But the terrible toll that drugs have taken on my family is still with me, my brother Douglas is incapacitated from several strokes he suffered while using drugs, his quality of live has been changed forever, I just thank God that he was not taken from us. And the toll in lives, young lives that were snuffed out from the violence around the city, as families wonder what life would have been like for their lost loved ones, to have seen these slain people grow to adulthood, for them to have children, perhaps marry. We will never know what contribution they could have made to humanity, all we have are memories of them, and my brother William who still live a tortured existence hooked on drugs as he burdens my mother and the rest of the family, like I once did. And of course my nephew Omar, his life will never be the same, because of a moment frozen in time, an act that he did not mean to do. These are the terrible tolls that drugs and alcohol take on our society, on our families and on our quality of life on a daily basis. Are we powerless to stop this self inflicted genocide, or to apathetic? These questions must be answered by all of us if we are to continue to grow as a people and as a society, the clock is ticking. The use of drugs has had an unchangeable effect on my family and others like us, we have lost loved ones, William Blake, James Langston, both died at the age of sixteen years old. We will never know what they might have grown up to be if given the chance, perhaps they would have made major contributions to society, we will never know now, but we can keep them in our memories. All of the people of our city have either suffered personal loss or knows someone that has suffered personal loss due too this drug epidemic. I think that there are too many people being hurt by the same things; we have to do something about this.

17

Death Takes No Holiday.

Nevertheless I have lost something. A part of me never recovered. I was an artist and that part of me seems to be gone. My long term memory has been affected, I cannot remember certain parts of my childhood. I struggle with personal relationships. I don't have as much to give to another human being. But the Millennium Foundation Inc. has allowed me to reach out to my fellow human beings, I now realize that the struggle to change our society must come from all members of our society; we cannot hide from that anymore. I do not have the same interest in sports, or other things that I had before. The drugs have truly had a negative effect on my personality, as well as a positive effect. Every day I wake up, I have to make a conscious decision not to use drugs, to fight off the demons that reside in me, personal and otherwise. Nevertheless do not feel sorry for me, but learn to have compassion for all the sick addicts that are still out there suffering. Because you see, I would not trade this person who I am for anyone else. The lessons learned the appreciation of life, my daughter, my family, all these thing is new to me, and I enjoy them. For the first time I fell well about myself and my self confidence has grown, so a trade off has taken place, you decide which is better, I already have. I grow stronger each day, and now have the confidence to achieve my goals and set goals in life.

I took off two years from work to invest in real estate and fulfill my dreams of being financially independent, I made some investments, both good and bad, and now I own a couple of home. Nevertheless I had to go back to work in 2006, I was put into a financial bind by a contractor who stole a large sum of money that was supposed to go toward the rehab of two properties. I cannot understand why he did it, but I now have to take this man to court to regain my money from this investment. About that time I went to work for Episcopal hospital, part of the Temple University Hospital Health System, I am doing the same work as I did before at Girard Medical Center, I working in the mental health field. I am sort of glad that I did go back to work, I had to much free time on my hands and it felt good to have that job again, plus I needed the money. I have met some wonderful people and enjoyed my job very much, my foundation, The Millennium Foundation Inc. was also sidetracked by not being able to acquire the needed grants to fund the programs that I wanted to run. I am now in the process of working to get funding, I have to do something, and the violence that has gripped Philadelphia is of epidemic proportions. This violence can claim anyone at anytime, as I and my family found out on July 28th, 2007. I had began to write articles for the Philadelphia Daily News about the spate of violent deaths in Philadelphia, young blacks were killing each other in record numbers in 2006 and again in 2007. Many of the deaths were over drugs and the victims and killers were getting younger and younger, no one seemed immune to the violence, young people, old people, babies, women and men. I knew that the outcome would be terrible, and continue to be so, so I wrote many articles about the violence that was fueled by the drugs, the guns and the ignorance. Then, on July 28th, 2007, I got a call from my sister telling me that my brother William had been stabbed in the neck at his home on 10th street and was taken to Temple University Hospital at Broad and Ontario Streets. At first I thought that it was not that serious, that it was just a false alarm, but it was much more, he had been mortally wounded. William was stabbed in the same house where I had lived out the last three years of my addiction; he still resided there after I had been clean for nine years, and toiling to get my life back together. Nevertheless my brother William kept on going, he was still caught up in the terrible problem of addiction, and he battled his demons until the end.

The literature of the Narcotics Anonymous states that addiction, any addiction will end up the same, jails, institutions or death and the literature is right. I tried to prepare myself for this day; the day when I would get the phone call telling me that my brother was dead, but even so when this day came, I found that I and my family were not prepared for the loss. How do you prepare for the death of a loved one? How do you steel yourself to face a tragedy such as the death of a sibling? How do you tell your mother and your father? We were faced with all of these questions, and I did not have the answer for them. It is a terrible thing to have to wait for someone to die, to be told by the doctors that they have done all that they can, that the injury is beyond the scope of their ability to repair. So we as a family gathered to wait at the hospital, we waited at Temple University Hospital in the waiting room of the trauma unit, and we were not alone, because other people were waiting to hear the fate of their loved ones just as we were. So much violence, so many lives affected like dominos, each event cascading and affecting so many other people, because that is what death is, it affects the lives of the family, and the friends and the survivors. My mother was out of town at the time, she was in Atlantic City when my brother William died, so we had to wait for her to come home and tell her, my mother collapsed and just repeated over and over my baby, my baby. A mother's love never diminishes with the passing of time, a mother's love never weakens no matter what we have become, or how we end, and a mother loves her child until the end.

So as a family we were once again faced with the terrible prospect of burying a loved one, my parents were once again forced to bury a child. It is truly horrible when parents outlive their children, I had witnessed this phenomenon almost ten years before when my brother Donald was killed, now we had to go through it all over again. The specter of death had reared its ugly head once again within my family and the guy who killed my brother was caught right away because my brother's girlfriend identified him to the police. It was someone that my brother knew, someone that he considered a friend. How did it come to this, what happened that caused this man to stab my brother in such a way that he mortally wounded him? I had to ask myself this over and over, just as I am sure that my family asked the same question, without any answers of course. God only knows the circumstances that can lead one human being to take another human beings life in such a vicious and brutal manner. I wish that I could go back and see what had happened that fateful day, to see the events that caused my Brother William's life to be snuffed out. I am so tired of the violence that seems to now be a part of our human experience, I am so tired of the every-day circumstances that lead to so many people to loose their lives here in Philadelphia, and we are all so tired. You almost dread a phone call from a loved one, because you feel that it could be bad news, and that is not the way it should be. I should always want to hear from my family, but the circumstances of life have made it so now that the late night phone call is a fear that never goes away

Now with the death of my brother, I am left with memories of him when we where growing up, I will remember his joke telling because he was such a jokester, I can remember his laughter, I remember his musical ability, man could he play some drums. I will remember him at his best, the way he was before his drug addiction, I will remember the bond that we shared growing up in that crowded bedroom, all six of the Glover brothers. The three double bunk beds, the three dress-ers, and the pile of dirty clothes that six young boys can accumulate in a week as we waited to go to the laundromat. I will remember the pain we shared in his house on Tenth Street. I remember the addiction that crippled us both and turned us into hopeless junkies, the misery, and the pain the suffering that we went through is bought back to the surface. The kindness he showed while I lived there with him and the meanness that he also showed is what made him who he was during that time and I cannot forget that.

The sacrifices of my mother to provide food for us, the sacrifices of both my parents, I have a picture of all ten of us, all the Glover brothers and sisters, taken long ago in the backyard of our house of Toronto Street. With a white sheet for a backdrop, we were posed by my father, it was Easter Sunday and we were on our way to church, all nine of my brothers and sisters and myself, my late brother Donald, my now incapacitated brother Douglas, and of course, my now late brother William. We all had no idea what fate awaited us; we were all so innocent, smiling for the camera, a moment forever frozen in time, the Glover children, the ten of us. My how things have changed, the effects of lives long lived, the effects of time and the effects of life and of death. I guess that it is that way for all of us, no; I know that it is that way for all of us. Memories are the most powerful results of living our lives, they are potent beyond description, they make us who we are, make no mistake about that!

You have no idea what I am talking about? You will one day!

The End

Epilogue:
Street Corner Symphony.

In writing this book, I had hoped it would be a catharsis for me, a continuation of the healing process within me, and a continuation of the self reparations and the healing that we as black people owe ourselves. It turned out to be much more than that! As I attempted to chronicle my life, and in turn the lives of my family and friends, make no mistake they are all intertwined, I had to deal with the results of my life and actions on a single humanistic level, something most of us do not or dare not do. The results were a chronological history that runs on a parallel line with the evolution of our society. This is the reality of generations of wrongs committed against us, and the results of these actions and the results of the self destructive behavior that we as black people have visited upon ourselves.

So I dedicate this book to my mother, Mozell R. Graham, who endured the pain and suffering that comes with her life being forever intertwined with ten offspring, and their offspring's offspring. The love, direction and faith that she gave us, along with all of my other family members, allowed me to find my way back, when God saw fit to let me. To my father, Robert L. Glover Sr., who tried to be a good father, but he was never given the proper tools to become I believe that a father is something that is learned, from your father to you, He never had a father and expressed as much to me, so he never learned to be a father, he did the best that he could, and now I finally have learned to love my father for who he is now and not blame him for what he was then. Also to my family, both the immediate and the extended, may we all continue to strive for the excellence in our everyday lives.

This book also deals with the ravages of our society and serves as an indictment of the Institutions of our society. It serves to remind us that the casualties of our action or our non-action are much more than chattel, these casualties have names, faces and they leave behind memories of them that will never be forgotten. To my late nephew James Langston who died at the age of sixteen. His was a life of misery and neglect, that we must all share the blame for, I most of all, for I was given the chance by God to make a difference in his life and did not. To William Blake, who also was killed at the age of sixteen, may he rest in peace finally and achieve the peace that he did not know in life. To my nephew Omar Burnett, who has been incarcerated for the last 10 years, may he one day be released to see his son and his cousin Sandra Glover, who was born right after his incarceration. To my Brother Donald L. Glover, we shared many adventures growing up, went through many things, and the memory of him that I will take to my grave is of him at his best, I thank God for letting us see that as a family, so that is how we will remember him, at his best, at his best. To my sister's Victoria R. Glover, and Robin L. Glover, who stepped in and raised my daughter when her mother and I were incapable, this is a debt that can never be repaid. To my sister Sharon Jones, who is always there, and epitomizes what family is about. To those in my family who I have wronged during my illness, stole from, I apologize to them. To the rest of my family, all of whom I love, who were there for me, thru my addiction. To all of the families that I grew up with, the friends that are no longer here, to the Smith's who lived across the street from my family on Toronto Street, to the Lee's Ernest and his family, he was like a brother too me. To the Sparrows and the Williams, to the Robinson's and the Browns, to the Cooks and the Harrell's, and to any and everybody that I may have forgotten, may they all remember the "Way".

And to Self Help Inc., the recovery institution that saved my life, to the counselors there who taught me not to be afraid to live and how to live again, to the pastor who ministered to us and to the ladies who ran the bible study every Wednesday. And to God, who reached his mighty hand out, stopped my spiral to hell, bought me back to tell others that there is hope. And to all the fallen, the still sick and the recovering sick, their families and to let their families know as I let my mother know, it was not their fault, it was mine.

Street Corner Symphony: Final Thoughts

As I finished my book and people read it, I found that this book touched a lot of people's lives, there was the young lady who bought a copy who was about to be wed to a man who was also in recovery like myself, she expressed to me how the book gave her a better understanding of what her fiancé was experiencing on a daily basis as he recovered from his illness that was his addiction. She even invited me to her wedding which I thought was nice. There were many stories and experiences that readers shared with me about growing up in Philadelphia. I had no idea that my story would touch so may people's lives, I had hoped that it would, but I still had no idea that it would. As I sit here writing these final thoughts, it is Monday, September 25th and a five year old child was shot too death on Sunday, September 24th in the Strawberry Mansion section of Philadelphia. She was shot along with her grandmother and another child, caught in crossfire between two groups of people shooting at each other. The gun violence in Philadelphia is unimaginable, as the memorials rise up on the street corners in Philadelphia Pennsylvania, a few teddy bears and a candle is all that is left to mark the spot where another young life has been snuffed out. A young person that was killed far too soon, before they could even taste what life has to offer. That person could have been the mayor of Philadelphia in their adult life that person could have found a cure for cancer, you never know what that young baby could have accomplished and we now will never know. My wish is that we can somehow reconnect with our young generation, the lost souls that roam our city streets and sell dugs and kill without impunity or remorse. These young people are us and we are them, although we sometimes forget that. These young people are the result of our neglect and of our apathy, we must embrace them with love, kindness and direction, only then will the killing stop. Everybody who lives in this city knows someone who was either killed, or lost someone too the violence, we must prepare ourselves for the battle that lies ahead, only through God can we gain the strength to show them the way out of their anger. The drugs and the guns that infest our streets must be and can be removed, it is not an easy task that lies before us, but it is winnable, we only need to take the first step, together.

And to my brother William V. Glover Sr., who was killed July 28th, 2007, may God grant him the peace that he so richly deserves; after all of the suffering that he has endured, may he see his brother Donald who also died far too soon. May William see his sons, William Jr. and James who also died far too young, may he see our Nana, our grand-fathers, our grandmother Mom-mom., Ruthie and Aunt Marion, and his cousins Kim and Danielle. And may they all welcome him home, and ease his pain and transition and may he smile, because he knows he is in a better place. And may all those that he has left behind, his children and grandchildren, parents and siblings rejoice for him for he has joined the kingdom of heaven.

Memorials in the City of Brotherly Love

I wake up from the weekend and read that another child is dead
It happens so often that it no longer blows my mind or my head
She was shot along with her grandmother while sitting in a car, a
victim of our Philadelphia's city streets
She was only three when she was killed; man that shit is way too
deep
So the first thing that we do in honor of her memory
We set up a memorial, that's the new thing to do, don't you see
To massage our guilt and our failure to this child, someone will get
a candle and a few teddy bears
When what we should be doing is smacking ourselves for not pre-
venting this tragedy and pulling out our hair
You see, there are far too many memorials sprinkled throughout
Philadelphia, the north south and west
As we mourn the loss of our young loved ones, to each family that
has lost them to that family they were the best
Testaments to the violence of the city of brotherly love
As our children continue to die, and are sent far too soon to heaven
above
You can't drive anywhere in this city without seeing these teddy
bear scenes
Every time that I see one it reminds that someone has died and it
shakes me to my very being
Children robbed of their lives, murdered by other children gone
astray
We got to get these guns off of the streets and these drugs off of the
corners, to end the violence that's the only way

Too end the violence and the teddy bears memorials that they both represent and are one and the same

For if we don't end this violence soon, there will be no one left and it will be to our shame

Soon we will have to get the military to on this city drop thousands of teddy bears

For there will be no left alive to place them, all will be dead and no one will be left to care

For we can do more to memorialize our dead children than putting out teddy bears and candles

We have to make sure that no more children are killed, on this problem we have got to get a handle

I know, I am tired too, but I will not let another child die

Too may are gone already, to them we have said goodbye

We must teach our young people that life is precious and to learn how to live

For killing and dying is easy, it is the gift of life that we must give

The day must come, when these teddy bears and candle memorials are a thing of the past

Or soon we won't have any children left, at this rate they just won't last

We need to see the last memorial of candles and teddy bears in our city

Or the next child killed might be mines or yours, don't you see

HUGGING THE BLOCK (LOCK STOCK & BARREL)

There seems to a new term for the new millennium, or maybe it's older than that

Hugging the block for young and old that seems to be where it is at

Get dressed in the morning and put on some gear, gear that is Phat

Because you'll be out there all day with no time to play and brother that's a fact

It's happening all over the city of Philadelphia, in the east, north, south and west

Out there in all types of weather, young black brothers in rain, sleet, snow and the sun trying to be the best

Out there to make the funds, for that fat dime, the new rides and the scriller

Cause if you don't get locked up or get killed, life can be the thriller

Out there all day and that's where you got to lay until that pack of drugs is done

You're not out there by yourself the man you work for will soon come by

Pull up in his new S.U.V. to make sure the count on that pack is right and you're not telling him a lie

It's hard to tell the players without a score card, but if you look closely you can tell

Rest assured that those who are hugging the block are in a living hell

It's just how you look at it I guess to determine your place in this mess

There are degrees of victimization, the degree you are responsible for you will have to decide for yourself

Where you fit in are you a player are you a smoker, or are you hooking to make ends meet

Rest assured that if you're out there you are a victim to some degree
How did all this happen aren't nobody working? No jobs to be found
or had
But that's no excuse for the things we do that cause us as a people to
go bad
You see we have lost it, it seems that the battles over, hope is gone and
these are the end of days
But we can still turn it around we just got to get our young people to
stop hugging the block
Lock Stock and Barrel

www.ingramcontent.com/pod-product-compliance
Lightning Source LLC
Chambersburg PA
CBHW020418290526
45785CB00002B/622